To Dear Marie & Norris,

A preview for your Nov 91 trip
And our 1992 Board Meeting.

Much love

Pram Senanayake

Sept 30th 1991.

TREASURES OF CHINA

TREASURES OF
China

Reader's Digest

Treasures of China —
An Armchair Journey to 352 Legendary Landmarks

Based on the book first published in Chinese in Hong Kong, Taiwan,
Malaysia and Singapore as '' 中國名勝古蹟 ''

Chief Editor: *Mein-ven Lee*
Art Director: *Roger S.F. Chung*
Production Director: *Natale Bauducco*
Art Editor: *Charn-wing Chan*
Staff Editor: *Stella S.Y. See*
Editiorial Assistant: *Kai-ching Tam, Po-ming Cheung, Sum-ching Wong.*

ISBN NO. 0-89577-325-2

Contents

Part of The Great Wall at Badaling, northwest of Beijing

The Northern Region

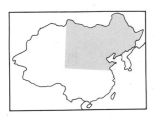

The rise of China as a distinct nation from a series of warring tribes is attributed to the power and aspiration of the Qin (Chin) dynasty of rulers nearly 2,200 years ago. The struggle for unity was momentous enough, but perhaps the most spectacular accomplishment was that of the first Qin emperor (Qinshihuangdi), who succeeded to the throne in 221 BC. To protect the infant nation from barbarian attack from the far north he began work on that monumental and abiding symbol of Chinese civilisation, the Great Wall, an immense "Maginot Line" of brick, packed mud and stone that was eventually to stretch some 6,000 kilometres across the Yellow River Valley and North China Plain to the Liaodong Peninsula.

It was a remarkable engineering feat and a colossal human achievement, with upwards of 500,000 peasant labourers pressed into work; but it also broke the back of the Qin rule. There was so much suffering and loss of life among the conscripts that, along with other painful and disruptive birth-pangs of the new society, it led to the overthrow of the dynasty in 207 BC, four years after Qinshihuangdi's death.

Strictly speaking, this region refers to all areas north of the Great Wall, including the northeast and Inner Mongolia, as well as Chengde and Yinchuan. It is the cradle of the Manchus, the "barbarians" who eventually overran China in the 17th century and established what was to become the last of China's imperial dynasties. The region is bounded to the north, east and southeast by four main rivers, the Heilong, Wusuli, Tumen and Yalu, and within the territories that they form there are four principal mountain ranges, the Qian, Changbai, Da Hinggan Ling and Xiao Hinggan Ling . Of these, Changbai sports the most dramatic scenery. Its main peak, Baitou, the tallest in the northeast, is capped with snow all the year round, and on its upper slopes lies the beautiful and moody Sky Lake (Tianchi), a huge volcanic crater-lake surrounded by 16 precipitous mountain peaks, that can be beautifully serene one day and a maelstrom of high winds and crashing waves the next.

The Changbai Range is also the source of another important river of the northeast, the Songhua, the main tributary of the Heilong. Winding through some 60 percent of the territory, the Songhua feeds two of the most attractive cities of the area — Jilin, the "river city", famous for its frozen "tree hangings" in winter and its three nearby lakes, and Harbin, which is completely ice-bound throughout the long winter months. Harbin (its name is a corruption of a Jurchen phrase for "honour" and "great reputation") is celebrated for its beautiful Spring Festival, when the streets are lit at night with ice-lanterns and ice and snow sculptures are displayed in its parks.

Shenyang, formerly Mukden, the capital of Liaoning Province, was once China's imperial capital — the founding emperor of the Manchu Qing dynasty (1644-1911) established his court there — and although the seat of rule was later returned to Beijing the city has fared none the worse for it. Shenyang has continued to grow and prosper, and is endowed with imperial architecture — the Imperial Palace, imperial mausoleums of Taizu and Taizong, and some 70 other courts and administrative buildings — which is among the most extensive and best preserved in China and ranks with the Forbidden City in Beijing.

By contrast the western area of the northeast, beyond the Daxing'an Range, is a seemingly boundless prairie dotted here and there with dense forests — the Mongolian tableland. Lying about 1,000 metres above sea-level, this is a land of sweeping plains, fierce summer and winter temperatures and nomadic Mongolian "cowboys" who live in felt tents, follow Tibetan lamaism, ride swift ponies and tend sheep, goats and cattle — "The sky so blue, the field so vast", as an old Chinese poem describes it. "When the wind blows the grass bows low, baring the sheep and cattle below." With all this grassland it is not surprising that the capital city of Inner Mongolia, Huhehaote (Huhhot), is also known as the "green city". It is also a treasure house of Tibetan Buddhist architecture, featuring several lamaseries, or monasteries, filled with finely executed sculptures, murals and frescoes.

Mohe

This, the northernmost outpost of China, is also called the "Arctic City" because of its bitterly cold winter climate. Its people call it the town of the "White Night" — for the time of the annual summer solstice when darkness closes in for only an hour or two before and after midnight. But its most dramatic feature is its natural *son et lumière* of the Aurora Borealis, the Northern Lights, when a small ring of light appears to the north of the city, expands until it literally fills the sky with colour, then retreats and disappears to the east.

◁

Zhenbao Dao (Damansky Island)

One of the major tributaries of the Heilong, the Wusuli River is a strategic one for it serves as a boundary between China and the Soviet Union. It is also one of the coldest places in China, with the temperature often plunging to minus 30°C in winter.

This river measures 890 kilometres in length, and flows through an area of 190,000 square kilometres of fertile land of virgin forests, mineral resources and agricultural products such as soya bean curd sorghum.

Zhenbao is a blunt finger of land two kilometres long, jutting out from the Chinese side of the Wusuli. Eroded by the river water, the connecting strip of land has been submerged. Thus

Zhenbao becomes an island when the river is high. However, land emerges during the dry summer season when the water level is low, connecting it once again to the mainland. It is an important fishing centre, and even in the coldest months when the Wusuli is frozen over, lines are cast Eskimo-style through the ice. In the autumn the river abounds with sturgeon and maha which are sometimes four to five metres

Five Connected Lakes

Between 1719 and 1721, huge volcanic eruptions tore at the mountains in the upper reaches of the River Bai, about 22 kilometres north of Dedu County in Heilongjiang Province. Masses of lava flooded and crashed into the river, damming it and forming one of China's most dramatic scenic spots, the Five Connected Lakes. From the vantage point of one of the mountains, Laohei, these lakes tumble through the craggy folds of the landscape like a string of blue gems. Surrounding them are no less than 24 active volcanoes, some of them smoothed away by the elements and others with distinctive cone-shaped peaks. This "Museum of Volcanoes", as it is known, has long been a popular hot springs resort. Not only did the lava flows create the lakes, they also divided the lower reaches of the Bai River into two streams — the Shilong He (Stone Dragon River) to the east, and to the west the Yaoquan He, or Medicinal Spring River.

On another local mountain, Huoshao, the lava flows not only cooled into a natural monstrosity of charred rocks and huge fissures, but carried on to form a "stone dragon" sprawling for several kilometres across the adjacent hills. Viewed from a distance this "dragon" looks more like a turbulent river, its waters caught and frozen in a split-second of time. But at close range, the lava has settled and twisted into weird shapes that resemble tigers, elephants, horses and giant lizards. ▽

in length, weigh 700 to 800 kilograms and have been known to gather in such staggering numbers to spawn that, as the *Heilongjiang Gazette* has observed, "their density was so great that local people would occasionally walk on them to cross the river." △

Dongzheng Church

Russian priests established the Dongzheng (Eastern Orthodox) Church in Harbin in 1899 — a magnificent domed, Byzantine structure and the finest of some 17 churches that they eventually built in the northeast. It still stands today, a reminder of the tumultuous struggles of the past and a witness to that most crucial of all struggles in Chinese history — the extent to which the Chinese have been willing to tolerate outside influence. Western religion was swept away once again in the 1949 communist revolution, and all foreign thought was rejected entirely during the violent cultural revolution of the late 1960s. Now, in its dramatic swing toward modernisation and technological competition with the West, China's doors are open again and a degree of religious tolerance is again being allowed. But so too is a far more marked, and perhaps premeditated, tolerance of Confucianism — the abiding ethic of Chinese society — and it would be reckless indeed to predict that places of worship such as Harbin's Dongzheng Church will remain much more than an architectural relic.

▽

Xingkai Lake

Lying on the border between northeastern China and the USSR, the Xingkai Lake actually forms the boundary between the two socialist giants. In a treaty signed in 1860 between Beijing and Moscow, a line was drawn midway between the north and the south, and today more than half of the lake's area lies in the USSR. The lake was formed when the land here subsided after a volcanic eruption. "Xingkai" in Manchurian means "water flowing down from higher grounds". The lake is 69 metres above sea level, has an area of 4,380 square kilometres and some areas of it are 10 metres deep. Nine rivers flow into it before it empties itself into the Wusuli River on the northeast. A smaller lake called Little Xingkai, is linked to the larger lake during flood time. The former lies entirely within Chinese territory. Xingkai Lake was called Meituo Lake during the Tang dynasty, named after the fish that flourished there. Nowadays, many different species of freshwater fish continue to be harvested, including sturgeon and freshwater porpoise. During the cold season, the lake freezes into a vast expanse of snow-brushed ice.

▽

Taiyang Island

The Taiyang Dao, or Sun Island, is a 10 square kilometre shoal on the Songhua River at Harbin, neatly landscaped with parklands, flowering shrubs and trees to serve as the city's main summer resort. With its spacious gardens and riverside groves of willow trees, it adds lustre to Harbin's long-standing reputation as the "jade" mounted on the shimmering silver necklace of the Songhua. ◁

Jingbo Lake

Jingbo Lake is another popular, though far more magnificent, northeastern resort — the largest dammed lake in China. Situated 50 kilometres southwest of Ning'an County in Heilongjiang on the upper reaches of the Mudan (Peony) River, it is 45 kilometres long and six kilometres wide and covers an area of 90 square kilometres. Its banks lie under high peaks and craggy walls, some of which hang in sheer precipices over the water.

These cliffs, peaks and scenic spots provide a number of spectacular viewpoints, called the Eight Sights of Jingbo — the Great Gu Mountain, Little Gu Mountain, Baishilazi, Laoguanlazi, Zhenzhumen, Chengqianglazi, Daoshi Mountain and the Diaoshuilou Waterfall. △

16

North Mountain (Bei Shan)

A much more illustrious and respected Chinese leader is enshrined in the Guandi Temple at Bei Shan, an almost sacred mountain resort in northwest Jilin Province. In this, the oldest of serveral temples built into the slopes of the area's two major peaks, the main shrine hall houses a towering image of General Guan Yu of the Shu Han dynasty (AD 221-263), during which the early attempts to unite China into a nation-state were consolidated and completed and the first state records systematised.

Alongside this military strongman there are images of his most powerful lieutenants, Guan Ping and Zhou Cang. In another temple, Yaowang, also called Sanhuang, there are three huge shrine halls devoted to other earthly and mythical heroes of Chinese culture — the Heavenly King, Earthly King, King of Humans and Sun Simiao, the King of Medicine. The images of some of the most famous pioneers of Chinese medicine, including Hua Tuo, Zhang Zhongjing, Li Dongyuan and Wu Qibo, are also there to be worshipped. Below the temples are two beautiful artificial lakes which are covered with lotus blossoms and pleasure boats during the summer and ice-bound for skating in the winter months.
▽

Manchuguo Palace

Of all the foreign challenges and incursions suffered by China, none is regarded as more savage and infamous than that of the Japanese occupation of the early 1930s. Emboldened by their stunning naval triumph over the Russians in 1904-5, their occupation of Formosa (Taiwan) and annexation of Korea, the Japanese invaded Manchuria in 1931, booted out the remnants of Russian influence and established a puppet government of "Manchuguo" (Manchukuo) under the last, deposed emperor of China, Henry Pu Yi. Here, visitors can see where he banqueted foreign diplomats and received the real power behind the Manchuguo throne, the commander-in-chief of the Japanese Guandong army. ◁

Songhua River

This mighty river is typical of much of the majesty of the northeast — no less than 1,840 kilometres long and flowing through more than half a million square kilometres of largely untamed land. Yet it is actually only a tributary, albeit the largest, of an even bigger river, the Heilong. And it has a benign and even touching aspect to its character: in the wintertime, when the

temperature can drop to as low as minus 30°C, and the river is ice-bound for up to five months at a time, a section of its waters around the Fengman Hydroelectric Power Station near Jilin remains free of ice, warmed by heated waste from the plant. Vapour rises from the river surface, condenses, then settles and freezes on the branches of willow trees that line the bank for miles. The result is an exquisite fairyland effect that the Chinese call "shu gua" or tree hangings, and which the more poetic have hailed as "jade trees with silver branches". Since the time of the Qing dynasty ice lanterns have been a popular folk art of the area, hung under the snow-packed eaves of homes and sometimes lit with candles.

Elsewhere, and on the more mundane level, the Songhua flows through the most extensive and possibly richest of China's wildernesses. It contains untouched forests that will one day yield lumber amounting to several billion cubic metres. Coal, gold, copper, iron and other minerals abound. The Songhua's fertile river basin produces soyabeans, corn, sorghum, cotton, tobacco and orchard fruits, and the river is also rich in freshwater fish, particularly carp, of which around 40 million kilograms are caught each year.

Songhua Lake

Lying on the upper reaches of one of the two main tributaries that feed the Songhua River, Songhua Lake is a popular tourist spot whose waters are dotted with dinghies and sailboats in summer and whose icy surface swishes with sleighs and skates in the winter season. As with most of the lakes of the northeast, it is surrounded by mountain peaks and forests and its shoreline is pitted with quiet and secluded bays and beaches. It also has its own islet, Wuhu, or Five Tigers, which is a favourite fishing spot.

But for all its beauty, Songhua Lake is also a strategic part of the industrial infrastructure of the northeast. It is a vast reservoir, almost an inland sea, with its waters stretching some 200 kilometres to the boundary of Huadian County; and it feeds the Fengman Hydroelectric Power Station which was built during the Japanese occupation. It is also well stocked with freshwater fish and provides irrigation to surrounding croplands.   ▷

Jilin Cathedral

Roman Catholicism was first introduced into China in 1508 at the waning end of the "glorious" Ming dynasty, and it appeared to have perhaps the best hope of all foreign religions of taking root and flourishing in the hitherto Buddhist Middle Kingdom.

Though suppressed in China during the 18th and early 19th centuries Catholicism nevertheless survived, and in 1682 it was able to find root in the northeast where great places of worship such as the Jilin Cathedral were built, many of them like this cathedral an almost perfect transplant of European Gothic architecture. In 1838, with the British and European navies and armed merchantmen forcing the Qing dynasty to its knees, an independent diocese was established in the region under Bishop Fang Ruowang, and it lasted for more than 30 years. In 1905 the Jilin Diocese was placed under the supervision of the French.   △

Longtan Mountain

Longtan is one of four great mountains of Jilin Province, yet probably took its name from a rather modest, nondescript pond called Longtan that nestles on its northwestern slope. But there's more to that pond than immediately meets the eye. On moonlit nights, when its waters are clear and placid, it is a perfect spot in which to enjoy one of the most poetic of Chinese relaxations — simply studying the moon, or its reflection.

The pond has another name, Shui-lao (Water Prison), referring to a legend in which an evil dragon reposed deep down in its waters, chained to a tree on its bank. Whenever the chain was pulled, so the story goes, a storm broke across the pond, whipping its surface into great turbulence. On top of Longtan Mountain stands an ancient walled city believed to be founded by the Gaojuli, a tribal state whose misty history predates Chinese nationhood. The wall has an observation tower at each of its four corners and from the southern tower visitors can view the entire city of Jilin. ◁

Changbai Mountain

This huge volcanic mountain range, stretching from southeast Jilin Province to the northern part of the Korean Peninsula, is one of the great natural treasures of China. It is rich in beauty, abounds with exotic wildlife and is a major source of ingredients for one of the most complex and most valued institutions of Chinese culture — herbal medicine.

Chinese historians attribute the birth of Chinese medicine to a legendary emperor, Shen Nong, who is said to have reigned some 5,000 years ago and to have become fascinated by the apparent medicinal properties of various plants. "Shen Nong tested the myriad herbs," wrote the Han dynasty historian, Sima Qian (Ssu-ma Chien), "and so the art of medicine was born." That art has developed over the centuries into an immense pharmacopoeia of potions, powders, pills, salves, tonics and other remedies taken from plants or from animals and reptiles.

Changbai Mountain was once an active volcano, and while it has erupted twice in relatively modern times — in the 17th and 18th centuries — it is now regarded as dormant. It features a group of 72 lakes formed from volcanic craters, the largest being the spectacular Sky Lake (Tian Chi). △

Sea of Forests (Linhai)

The Chinese reverence for nature and myth is reflected in the pictures they have painted of forests that rear up and roll and swell, and the leafy waves that lift and crest for as far as the eye can see around the beautifully named Sky Lake, in the heart of the Changbai Mountain Range. The forests sweep to the east, west and north of the lake in Antu, Fusong and Changbai counties, and cover a total area of about 4,000 sqare kilometres. Their character and category change according to the altitude: up to 1,000 metres the trees are largely leaf-shedding pines, willow and birch; at 1,000 to 1,800 metres lies the needle birch zone and the slopes are thick with evergreen pines and firs; at the highest altitude, the Yuehualin Zone at 1,800 to 2,000 metres, the steep gradients and cold, windy conditions have made the tree-cover more stunted and sparse. ◁

Sky Lake (Tian Chi)

Millions of years ago the Changbai Mountain ("Snow-capped Mountains") thundered and rocked with almost continuous volcanic eruptions. The legacy of that prehistoric violence is a series of 60 deep craters which have since filled with water to form the beautiful and brooding Sky Lake, south of Baihe County in Jilin Province. It is one of the world's most magnificent sights, lying just over 2,000 metres above sea-level, covering an area of 9.2 square kilometres, its waters more than 300 metres deep in some places and surrounded by 16 mountain peaks.

In fine weather the lake is so serene and its waters so clear that you can see the rocks many fathoms down on its bed. But the weather can change very abruptly, and strong winds can whip the face of the lake into a rage of metre-high waves. In the winter months the mood changes again, the frozen surface mirroring the mountain peaks around it. △

Jade Emperor Mansion

Located in northwest Jilin, the Jade Emperor Mansion was built in 1774 and renovated in 1926. The grounds were landscaped to blend with the original terrain, and the temple complex was built on two levels and designed to conform to the concept of "symmetry with a central axis". The mansion's front section consists of a main gate, a bell tower, a drum tower, an Ancestral Master temple, a Guanyin shrine, a Laolang shrine and a Huxian hall. Inside the main gate stand the Four Heavenly Kings: Huguo on the east, Zengzhang on the south, Guangmu on the west and Duowen on the north. Then comes a wooden arch with a horizontal plaque bearing the characters "Tian Xia Di Yi Jiang Shan" meaning "the foremost country in the world".

The rear section, Duoyun Hall, the mansion's main centre of worship, houses the Jade King, who is considered by the Taoists to be the highest authority of heaven. Two minor gods flank the statue, Thousand-mile Eye and Favourable-wind Ear, and 28 multi-coloured astrological gods decorate the walls. ◁

Thousand Mountains (Qian Shan)

Located east of Anshan in Liaoning Province, the Qian is a range of almost a thousand mountain peaks. In ancient times it was called "Thousand Lotus Blossoms Mountain" because the peaks were seen as a vast cluster of lotus blooms on a pond; and, not surprisingly, its dramatic beauty and isolation have made it a holy place, revered in poetry and song:

If you do not ascend the Immortal's Terrace,
Your visit to Qian Mountains is wasted.
Once you are on top of the Immortal's Terrace,
You can see the Bo Sea in the east."

Indeed, the Immortal's Terrace is the highest spot, 708 metres to its peak, where the characters "Xian Ren Tai", carved into a huge rock, proclaim its name. On the second highest peak, Wufo, five stone Buddha images await those of the faithful who can complete the gruelling climb. The guide to Thousand Mountains lists no less than 164 places of interest, including many Buddhist and Taoist monasteries and temples. Some of the most striking ones were built in the early part of the Manchu Qing dynasty — the largest of them, the Wuliang Monastery, featuring ornate shrines to the gods. ◁ △

Zhao Tombs

The Manchu dynasty, which ruled China from 1644 until the republican revolution of 1912, seized power from the waning Mings with a fierce military alliance of peoples from "beyond the Great Wall". Yet the name Manchu did not really come into being until the imperial throne had been taken, and the dynasty itself represented the triumph of a war machine created by a mixture of Mongol pastoralists, urban traders, hunters and fishermen welded together in the 17th century by a chieftain of the primitive Tungu tribe. Once in power, this "Manchu" culture was rapidly diluted and assimilated by the predominant Han or "Chinese" culture of the south.

Zhao Tombs, also known as North Tombs (Bei Ling), stand in the city of Shenyang as a memorial to the military success of the Manchus. It is the tomb of the Manchu warlord Taizong, who led the "barbarian" alliance to the very foot of the imperial throne. Construction of the tomb began in 1643, the year before the Manchus took power, and it was completed in 1651. It was extended into an imperial mausoleum during the reigns of Taizong's successors, the Emperors Shunzhi (1644-1661), Qianlong (1736-1796) and Jiaqing (1796-1820).

Surrounded by massive stone walls, the entire burial complex covers 180,000 square metres and includes finely carved arches, ornamental pillars, stone lions, bridges, ceremonial pavilions and the magnificent Longen shrine hall, with its ornately carved colonnades and yellow-glazed tile roof.

Fu Tombs

Another Manchu emperor, Taizu, was buried with his queen in the Fu Tombs in the eastern suburbs of Shenyang. Started in 1629 and completed in the same year as Taizong's tomb, they lie on the thickly wooded bank of the Hun River with the Tianzhu Mountain behind them.

Though the tombs' architecture and layout are quite different from Taizong's resting place, they include the usual arches, bridges, ceremonial pavilions and carved animals — and the divine touch of the Manchu emperors.

The building complex faces south and is surrounded by massive walls. In the middle of the south wall is the main gate which is flanked by glazed tiles decorated with a dragon motif.

On both sides of the open porch of the main gate there are *Xiama*, or "alight from horse" tablets that are found in most imperial burial places. "All officials below the rank of prince should dismount here," they warn. The Xiama at this tomb were origi- nally inscriptions in wood, but these were replaced with stone in 1783 when Emperor Qianlong visited the tombs to pay his respects.

The *pailou*, or main arch, pictured above, has a double-eaved roof sucovered by yellow glazed tiles. Beyond the arch stands a stele. The inscription on it is a eulogy to the greatness of the imperial ancestors in the calligraphy of Emperor Kangxi.

To the south of the tombs' pailou, there are 108 terraced steps, each of them built of green bricks and supported by a planet to symbolise the imperial "mandate from heaven". A marble pavilion in the north wall bears the inscription "Taizu Gaohuangdi Zhi Ling" (Tomb of Emperor Gao, Taizhu) — a personal tribute from Emperor Kangxi who ruled from 1662 to 1723.

On a platform in the middle of the walled structure stands the sacrificial hall (picture on right).

The Ancient Palace

Though the Tungu tribal chieftan, Nuerhachi, is said to have first gathered together the Manchu military alliance, the warlord Huang Taiji is credited with the first major step toward what was envisioned as Manchu nationhood and empire. It was he, so the records say, who conquered and united the entire northeast, and for this he was installed as king in Chongzheng Hall, one of more than 70 great pavilions and courts in the Ancient Palace in Shenyang.

In scale and architecture this palace rivals the Forbidden City in Beijing. Construction began in 1625 and was completed in 1636; and to any visitor from the south, it must have stood as a mighty portent of the imperial conquest that was to come. It became the seat of power of all the early Manchu kings — Taizong and Taizu among them — and was renovated an extended by the Emperors Kangxi and Qianglong in the succeeding era of imperial triumph.

Built in three sections, each of them containing separate courts with their own halls, shrines and pavilions, the palace features the beautiful three-storey Fenghuang (Phoenix) Mansion, a royal banqueting hall whose uppermost floor offers a panoramic view of modern Shenyang. Another mansion, Wensu, houses two voluminous and academically invaluable anthologies of Manchu history. ▽

Dazheng Hall and Shiwang Pavilions

The Dazheng Hall and Shiwang Pavilions form the east section of the Ancient Palace, and, more than anything else, commemorate the militaristic nature of the Manchus. The Dazheng Hall, an eight-sided double-eaved wooden structure crowned with a golden dragon, has a row of five pavilions on each side of it, extending from north to south, each built of blue-green bricks and supported by red pillars. The effect is very much like two lines of army tents guarding the commander-in-chief — a symbol of the success of the Qing dynasty's founder, Emperor Shunzhi, who spent the better part of his life on the battlefield and was blessed with the loyal support of his generals.

The Shiwang Pavilions is where the ten most important lieutenants of the Manchu king — two princes and eight ministers — met each day to plan the campaign of military strategy and political intrigue that was aimed at imperial rule. The complex, actually a series of inter-connected rooms, is now a museum of Manchu armour, carriages, military costume, campaign banners and weapons, including a sword that is said to have been worn by Emperor Qianlong and is still today, more than two centuries after his reign, untarnished.

◁ △

31

Mongol Temple

Although a distinctive school of Buddhism centred on the palace of the Dalai Lama in Lhasa, Tibetan lamaism is also widespread in Mongolia and Manchuria. In Inner Mongolia, lamaseries dot the sparsely inhabited grasslands, most of them a blend of Tibetan and Han Chinese architectural styles. Two fine examples are Wusutu Temple and Xilitu Temple, erected during the Ming dynasty and still remarkably well preserved after a series of renovations. Temples built during the later Qing rule include those at Meidai, Bailing and Beizi. ◁

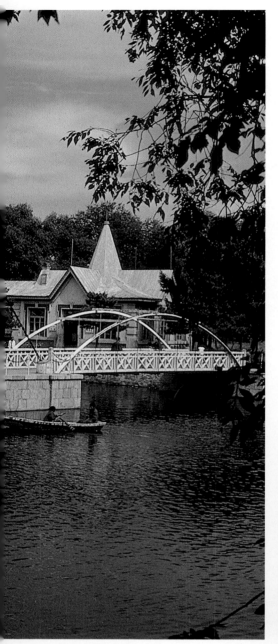

Yalu River Bridge

The Yalu River, a tributary of the Nen River flowing from the eastern slopes of the Daxing'an Range, was one of the strategic and most emotive keywords of a conflict that almost plunged East Asia and the rest of the world into a third global war. It was the point at which thousands of Chinese troops poured across the northeast Chinese border in the Korean War, supporting the communist North Koreans against the American-backed United Nations forces defending the south.

At Zhalantun a 50-metre suspension bridge spans the Yalu, its central section supported by massive steel chains that pass through the tops of its columns. Its engineering is so delicately balanced that a touch of the hand is enough to swing the central span like a cradle. Beyond the bridge, the Yalu widens so that it looks more like a lake than a river. Along its lower eastern reaches its waters form a series of bow-shaped lakes which, viewed from the mountains, are like glittering crescent moons. ◁

Zhalantun

Located on the eastern slope of the Daxing'an Range, which runs northeast to southwest across Inner Mongolia, Zhalantun is a small hillside town inhabited by a mixture of Han Chinese and several ethnic minorities, including Mongols and Koreans. It is a place of dramatic beauty, a city literally sprouting like an oasis out of the empty plain. With the Yalu River flowing through its parks and meadows, it has been described as the Hangzhou (Hangchow) of the north. ▷

Dajingtang

This, the principal building or Great Sutra Hall of the Xilitu Temple, has walls inlaid with peacock-blue tiles with gilded silver decorations. The roof is even more ornate, mounted with a gilded vase (*baoping*), Tibetan prayer-wheel, a flying dragon and a deer — all cast in copper and contrasting with the red door and polychrome painting below. Eight Tibetan columns support the front porch. The two-storey building is where the lamas gather to chant the Buddhist scriptures. ▽

Xilitu Temple

The Xilitu Temple, situated in the old wall of Huhehaote, was built in the Ming dynasty but enlarged over the years until, in the early Qing reign, it included a shrine hall with eight columns. When Emperor Kangxì returned from a military expedition to the western frontiers he visited the temple, bestowed gifts of sutras, rosaries and weapons and gave it a Han name, the Yanshou Monastery. A tablet commemorating his victory is still standing in an eight-cornered pavilion, inscribed with details of his battles in Han, Manchu, Mongolian and Tibetan. As with most monasteries in the northeast, the architecture is principally Chinese with the main shrine hall and sutra hall in the Tibetan style. ▷

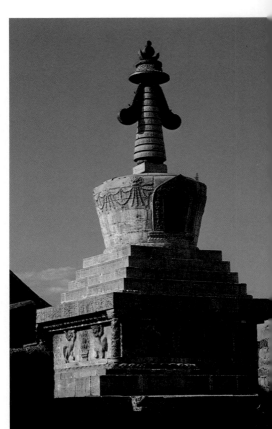

Sheli Pagoda

Buddhism spread to China from India in the first century AD, and faced a society which not only boasted an already long-established civilisation but considered itself the only truly civilised society on earth. It took a long and arduous struggle for the new belief to take root, and even then it survived largely because it was able to adapt to and complement China's traditional native teachings, Confucianism and Taoism, rather than attempting to usurp them.

The Chinese are thought to have first come into contact with Buddhism through central Asians travelling in from the north and northwest. Later, in the 7th to 10th centuries, it literally flooded in along with other religions and sects from the West across the deserts, mountains and steppes of that fabled Central Asian trade route, the Silk Road. And, alongside these other religions, it eventually came under the hammer of an imperial edict, issued in AD 845, declaring that all imported foreign influence had gone quite far enough.

But while chastened, Buddhism has survived, and in China's northeast there are many fine temples such as the Jingangzuo Sheli Pagoda near the old wall of Huhehaote (Hohhot) in Inner Mongolia which were built as late as the Qing dynasty and exhibit a mixture of Han, Mongol and Tibetan Buddhist influences typical of this frontier region. Sheli Pagoda is the only section of the much larger Cideng (popularly known as Five Tower) Monastery that has managed to withstand the ravages of time. It consists of five square-shaped brick and stone towers, faced with glazed tiles, mounted upon a stone base — an example of a particularly rare form of Buddhist architecture.

△

Huayan Sutra Pagoda

Located in the eastern section of Huhehaote City, the Huayan Sutra Pagoda goes by the far more formidable full name of Wanbu Huayan Jingta ("Ten Thousand Volumes of Avatamasake Sutra Pagoda"); but, mercifully, it is commonly called the White Tower. It is also a fine example of earlier Buddhist architecture, probably erected between AD 983 and 1031 in the era of Song refinement and enlightenment that followed the Tang dynasty's crackdown on "alien" religions. It is an eight-sided tower of wood and brick, seven storeys or 45 metres high — imposing even for the inspirational architecture of its time. It stands upon the site of what was formerly a monastery named Daxuanjiao, and within its walls there is a remarkable display of historical graffiti — inscribed by visitors as far back as the Jin dynasty (1115-1234) and written not only in Chinese but also Mongolian, Nuzhen, ancient Syrian and Persian. ▽

Zhaojun's Tomb

The tomb of Wang Zhaojun, a 33-metre high mound of loess (sandstone), stands on the south bank of the Dahei River nine kilometres south of Huhehaote.

Built originally, it's said, as the burial place of an imperial concubine, it has since been endowed with the power to cure infertility in women. The story has twisted and changed over the centuries but can be traced back to the quite simple tale of Wang Zhaojun, a girl from a good family, who was selected to live in the Han imperial court. A prince named Huhanye from the Xiongnu region came to visit the court and expressed his desire to marry the girl for the sake of closer ties with the imperial throne. Since then, the people of the Huhehaote region have believed that a pinch of soil taken from the grass-covered tomb will make childless women pregnant. △

Yan Shan Old Monastery

Tibet came under nominal Chinese suzereinty from the year 1700. Yet it was left free to practise lamaism, a school of Mahayana Buddhism, and its own politico-religious form of rule in which all power was in the hands of its spiritual leader, the Dalai Lama.

In China itself, Tibetan Buddhism has flourished for centuries throughout the northeast, surviving upheavals to remain the principal belief of the Mongolians and other ethnic groups of the region. There are lamaseries throughout the area that remain unscathed, and the Yin Shan Old Monastery, 100 kilometres north of Huhehaote, is one of them — set like a jewel in the boundless green satin of the Mongolian grasslands. ▷

Wudang Temple

Another grander example of Tibetan Buddhist architecture, the Wudang Lamasery, lies on a mountain slope 70 kilometres northwest of Baotou in Inner Mongolia. It is not only the sole surviving complete lamasery in the region, with more than 2,500 living units, classrooms, temples and halls of worship, it is also one of the main centres of lamaism in China. Built in 1749 by the Dalai Lama himself, its name in Mongolian means "Willow tree".

The temple is built in the traditional Tibetan style with monolithic white stone walls, but this rather forbidding simplicity gives way to striking colour inside the temples and schools. In the main hall, Suguqindu, for example, where the lamas gather to conduct prayers and the chanting of the scriptures, the columns are clad in colourfully woven pillar rugs, the floors are similarly carpeted and religious murals cover the walls. The two floors above the hall are filled with images of Sakyamuni and other Buddhist deities. In another hall, Queyilindu, the centre for

the teaching of the sutras, there is a bronze Sakyamuni figure 10 metres tall.

Other halls in the sprawling complex are schools for the teaching of astronomy and geography, medicine and the history and disciplines of lamaism. There is also a museum of sorts, the Dongkuoerdu Hall, displaying relics and personal effects left by seven Dalai Lamas who were in temporary residence here at various times in the past.　　　　△▷

Dazhao

The Dazhao Monastery in the old section of Huhehaote presents a different architectural picture of Chinese Lamaism, a blend of Chinese and Tibetan Buddhist design. Built in the Chinese style in 1580, it was extended during the reign of the Qing emperor Kangxi and the roof of the main shrine hall clad with yellow-glazed tiles. However, the main structure of the hall is distinctly Tibetan, a traditional double-storey white "fortress" design with a porch, sutra chamber and a Buddha shrine where the most valued possession of the lamasery is on display — an image of Sakyamuni cast entirely in silver. It is from this splendid statue that the lamasery takes its popular Chinese name, Silver Buddha Monastery.

◁

The Mongolian Pastures

For panorama, there is little to compare with the eastern expanses of the Inner Mongolian tableland — a flat green sea of pastureland stretching from horizon to horizon and broken only by an occasional cluster of sheep and cattle and yurts, the portable felt igloo-shaped tents of the nomads, and their wraiths of cooking smoke.

These Mongolian "cowboys", about one and a half million of whom live in Inner Mongolia, make their livelihood from breeding and raising flocks of sheep and goats and herds of cattle, horses and camels. They are ruddy, strong-faced people with high cheekbones and distinctive straight noses, and naturally they are expert horsemen.

There is evidence on this boundless pasture of the fear that these once-unconquerable mounted warriors struck into the hearts of their immediate neighbours and the Han Chinese to the south — two ancient walls, built

Hai Pagoda

One of the oldest and most interesting Buddhist structures in the northeast is the Hai Pagoda, or North Pagoda, in the city of Yinchuan. Although there is no actual record of the date of construction, a book written in the Ming reign says it was rebuilt in the 5th century by a local prince. There are later records, however, of its renovation after an earthquake between the reigns of the Qing emperors Kangxi and Qianlong.

Standing on a high and spacious square base, the pagoda is built entirely of brick and rises 11 storeys to a height of 54 metres. It has an unusual design: a broad ridge rises from the middle of each wall, occupying one-third of the wall surface, so that each of its four walls looks as though it is actually three. Viewed from a distance, this design creates an optical illusion in which the pagoda has 12 corners and 12 high windows shaped like Buddha niches. The structural lines are well defined, giving the building an austere and robust character. Its roof is a peach-shaped dome of green tiles. ▽

by the Nuzhens, the ancestors of the Manchus, probably to guard against Mongol attacks. Both are more than 100 kilometres long. One lies to the northwest of the region along the Ergun River to the west bank of the Lai Lake, and the other is in the southeast, running from the southern slopes of the Daxing'an Range to Solon. △

Zhijingyun Dyke

The Manchu emperor Kangxi, who reigned from 1662 to 1723, was not only a staunch military defender of the realm but a man of certain culture and refinement too. And when the Manchu rulers built their magnificent Imperial Summer Villa in Changdi much of Kangxi's artistic vision went into it. The Zhijingyun Dyke, a vast and beautiful series of pools and water-gardens modelled on the West Lake of Hangzhou, was laid in one of 36 scenic spots selected by the emperor himself. This charming blend of man-made ponds, dykes, islands and willow-lined promenades became the jewel in the crown of a palace garden covering no less than five million square metres — double the area of the Summer Palace in Beijing. The Chinese love of nature and their respect for what they see as the natural harmony of existence is reflected in the names they gave their gardens and pavilions. North of the Zhijingyun Dyke there lies, for example, the Misty Rain Mansion. ▷

Shuixin Pavilion (Lake Centre Pavilion)

This pavilion, lying north of the main palace area and south of Misty Rain Mansion, was once the watergate on the border of the lakes. In 1709, during extensive redevelopment of the summer villa grounds, the Silver Lake and Mirror Lake were added to the eastern fringe, along with three pavilions which Emperor Kangxi named collectively Lake Centre Pavilion. All three structures stand on bridges into which as many as eight watergates have been set. ◁

Heavy-Snow-on-South-Hill Pavilion

The Heavy-Snow-on-South-Hill Pavilion stands on a hilltop in the northwest section of the gardens with three other evocatively named buildings close to it: Surrounded-by-Hills-and-Clouds Pavilion, Two-North-Peaks-as-Pillows Pavilion and the Pointed-Peak-Setting-Sun Pavilion. The square Heavy-Snow Pavilion, with its winged, tent-like roof, was given its name by Kangxi and stands rather precariously on the edge of a bluff. The view from there is outstanding. ▽

Imperial Summer Villa

The Imperial Summer Villa, the biggest garden palace complex in China, was started in 1703 and took 87 years to complete. It was a summer resort for the Manchu Qing emperors and was also known as the Jehol Travelling Lodge or Li Palace. Its grounds, only 20 percent of which are lakes and gardens, and the rest hills, are guarded by a wall that runs 10 kilometres around the perimeter.

The villa itself includes the Central Palace, Pine-and-Crane Studio, East Palace and a residential complex known as Wanhesongfeng. As with all Chinese courts the architecture is elegant with one aim in mind — to promote peace and harmony. Bronze lions guard the outer gate and the main door to the compound proclaims its name in characters that are said to have been inscribed by the Emperor Kangxi himself. Visitors can view the Danpojingcheng ceremonial hall, built of wood from the nanmu tree, the emperor's bedchamber and a two-storey mansion in which the stairs form part of an artificial hill of rock. The decor of the entire palace complex is pleasantly free of ornate carvings, gilt or decorative painting — a purely rustic refuge from the summer dust-storms and political heat of court life in Beijing.

Misty Rain Mansion

As its name suggests, this mansion was specially designed for the enjoyment of mist and rain on the surrounding lakes and hills. Standing on the rise of Great Lotus Island, it was styled after a mansion of the same name on Mandarin Duck Island in South Lake, Zhejiang. It is a two-storey single-eaved building supported by red pillars and clad with green glazed tiles. Again, its name was bestowed by Emperor Kangxi, and it is inscribed in his own hand on a plaque on the upper floor.

The mansion's east side includes a three-room study which was the emperor's "book house" or reading room. The western section is called the Facing Hills Studio. Pavilions stand on three sides of the building, and the view includes the Ten-Thousand-Trees Garden, the Jehol Springs and Yongyou Monastery. The mansion and its gardens are at their best in the summer months when the lotuses are in bloom, the rain settles in a gossamer mist on the leafy pools and a smoky mist rises from the waters. ▽

Putuo Zongcheng Temple

Built in 1767, this lamasery is designed in a series of terraced steps up a broad hillside and is modelled on the seat of Tibetan Buddhism, the Potala Palace in Lhasa. It consists of some 40 buildings — shrines and dormitories for the monks — dominated from the crest of the hill by the monolithic Red Terrace, which houses the principal Wanfaguiyi Shrine. This huge structure is built on granite foundations, rises 43 metres high and has walls of pink and white stone. Its tapered roof, covered with copper fish-scale tiles, is one of the finest examples of Tibetan Buddhist architecture outside Tibet itself. ▷

Pule Temple

Completed in 1766 on a plain to the northeast of the Imperial Summer Villa, this pavilion-styled temple was where the Qing rulers received emissaries of the Kazakh and Burut tribes and other Central Asian minorities of China's northeast. It features a pavilion containing a stone tablet inscribed with the temple's history and said to have been written by Emperor Qianlong. Its second storey is roofed by a circular double-eaved pavilion styled on the Qinian Hall of the Temple of Heaven in Beijing. Inside this pavilion there is a three-dimensional mandala, at the centre of which is set a bronze sculpture of the Happy Buddha, a reincarnation of Avalokitesvara. The inside of the domed ceiling is decorated with seven concentric murals featuring dragon and phoenix motifs — both these mythical creatures ranked by ancient Chinese naturalists as leaders of the five grand divisions of the animal world — and at the centre there is another beautifully executed mural on the theme "two dragons playing with a pearl". ▽

The Thousand Hands and Thousand Eyes Bodhisattva

This statue, one of the biggest wooden Buddha images in the world, stands over 22 metres high and is constructed of five different timbers, elm, fir, pine, juniper and cypress. More than three tonnes of metal were also used to link and reinforce its torso and many limbs. The head alone weighs five and a half tonnes, and the weight of the entire image is estimated at a little under 125 tonnes. The statue has 42 arms, with each hand holding a sacred object and each palm containing an eye. The face has three eyes, symbolising the Buddha's ability to know the past, present and future. As a Bodhisattva, the image also represents a being whose essence has achieved wisdom but whose fate it is to undergo many rebirths, existing for the good and guidance of others, until eventually reaching Buddhahood. Above this image stands another 1.4-metre high Amitabha Buddha, also known as the Impersonal Buddha and believed to preside over the Paradise of the West where the souls of the pious may go to exist in a state of bliss. ◁

Puning Temple

An enormous, ornately decorated wooden Buddha dominates the main hall of the Puning Temple, built in 1755 to the northeast of the Imperial Summer Villa. It was commissioned and installed to commemorate a Qing Dynasty victory over rebellious Mongols supported by the Russians. A detailed account of the battle, the Conquest of Tian Mountain, is inscribed on stone tablets in Chinese, Mongolian, Manchurian and Tibetan in an adjacent yellow-tiled pavilion. Two other shrines feature an image of the Maitreya Buddha, or Future Buddha, and Sakyamuni, the Indian prince who, seeking to be emancipated from the sorrows and agonies of life, spent a penance of seven years in the shade of the sacred Bodhi tree to attain enlightenment.

The Puning Temple is essentially Tibetan, an imitation of the Samye Monastery, and its main hall, the Mahayana Pavilion, is more than 36 metres high and surrounded by small pagodas and pavilions symbolising the "Four Corners" and "Eight Minor Corners" of the universe as interpreted by the Buddhist scriptures. In other halls to the southwest of the pavilion the Qing emperors once rested and listened to Buddhist sermons. ▷

Xumi Fushou Temple

The Xumi Fushou Temple was built north of the Imperial Summer Villa in 1780 to accommodate the sixth Panchen Lama when he travelled from Tibet for the 70th birthday celebrations of the Qing emperor Qianlong. The temple is virtually a replica of the Trashilungpo Monastery in Kagaze, and its Chinese name is a translation meaning "with the longevity and well-being of Mount Xumi", a legendary mountain in Buddhist mythology. Occupying a total area of 37,000 square metres, the temple's architecture is mainly Tibetan, with certain details modified into Han style. Calligraphy by emperor Qianlong, indicating the name of the temple, adorns the entrance. The main hall where the sixth Panchen Lama gave his sermons is located on the top of the three-tiered Big Red Terrace, while the Lama's residence is located to the west. The temple also features, among other fanciful structures, a green-glazed Pagoda of Longevity, similar to the one in Xiangshan Park.

△

The Great Wall

Nothing can really compare with the immense human labour that history tells us was pressed over a period of many centuries into the construction and almost constant renovation and expansion of that greatest of monuments to Chinese civilisation, the Great Wall.

When it was first started during the Qin dynasty in the 3rd century BC, the emperor ordered the linking up of older tribal walls and some 500,000 peasants — among them many convicted criminals — were forced into labour. In the later interim and unstable rule of the Northern Wei (AD 386-534), another 300,000 people were put to work on a single section south of Datong. In AD 607-608, when north-south political divisions were still shaking the foundations of Chinese unity, a full one million people were pressed into further work. But all this paled completely against the many millions of labourers conscripted during the Ming dynasty to modernise, strengthen and extend the wall — this stage of the project alone taking more than 100 years to complete.

The result is nothing short of a human marvel, a man-made protective barrier that snakes a distance of 6,000 kilometres over and through the rumpled folds of the northern Chinese landscape from Shanhaiguan on the shores of the Bo Sea, through Hebei, Shanxi, Inner Mongolia, Shaanxi, Ningxia and Gansu Provinces until it reaches Jiayuguan in the arid west. It is a monument to the human spirit, and it is a memorial to immense human suffering. Many thousands died during each work campaign, of sickness, accident, exposure or simply the physical ordeal. Almost everything was done by hand, masses of hands passing from one to the other the raw materials — rock, earth, bricks, lime and timber — up mountainsides and along ridges to each work-site. Handcarts were used on flat land or gentle slopes and goats and donkeys sometimes hauled the bricks and lime, but otherwise it was harsh and unremitting human toil that built the one man-made feature of the earth's surface that can be seen from outer space.

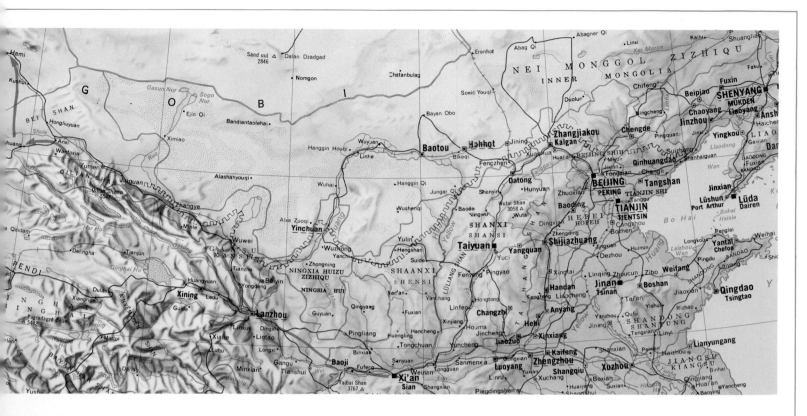

The Great Wall of the Warring Kingdoms

Long before the Great Wall itself was built, primitive defensive mounds and walls were thrown up here and there throughout northern China to protect tribal groups from surprise attack. According to ancient records the state of Chu built walls in the 7th century BC in the areas which are now Henan and Hubei Provinces.

The Great Wall of the Warring Kingdoms emerged from several defensive lines of tamped earth built by the various states, and it was these unconnected walls that were joined together and strengthened to form the first stage of the Great Wall in the Qin dynasty. Pictured below is the Qi wall, built in the 5th century BC in what is now the province of Shangdong. It runs from Pingyin in the west, around the northern slopes of Tai Mountain, and ends at the coast. ▽

Jiayuguan

The western reaches of the Great Wall terminate at a point to the southwest of Jiayuguan in the Gobi sands of Gansu Province. And it is here that the Ming emperor Taizu built the Tianxia Xiongguan (the "World's Greatest Fortress") in 1372 on the site of an earlier fortification that had been there since the time of the Han. It is said that the Ming engineers were so meticulous, and their specifications so exact, that when the new fort was completed only a single brick remained. It has since been proudly displayed in one of the fort's halls.

This well-preserved stronghold covers an area of 33,500 square metres, with a wall 10 metres high surrounding it. There are two gates, on the eastern and western corners, each built into

Watchtowers of the Great Wall

There were two types of watchtowers built along the Great Wall — *qiangtai* (wall towers) which were erected on the wall itself or jutted from its sides, and *ditai* (enemy towers) which were two-storey fortifications containing living quarters and arsenals and crenellated parapets. Many of these enemy towers can still be found along a 500 kilometre section of relatively intact wall in the northern part of Hebei Province. Designed by the Ming general Qi Jiguang, they were placed at short intervals, particularly between Juyongguan and Shanhaiguan. △

three-storey gatehouses with single-eaved half-hipped roofs. As with most of the Great Wall's fortified points, Jiayuguan straddles a strategic pass between the Qilian and Heli mountain ranges. It was also an important access for the overland caravans of the Silk Route. ◁ △ ▷

The Great Wall at Jinshan

One particularly well-defended stretch of the wall — now crumbling in many places — was built in 1570 by General Qi Jiguang to cover a series of low rolling hills at Jinshan. Because the open, gently rising terrain gave any enemy easy access to the Han hinterland, the wall along this 30 kilometre section was heavily strengthened and well fortified with watchtowers and beacon posts. ◁

Juyongguan

When the first emperor of Qin completed the first stage of the Great Wall's construction he found he had another problem on his hands — many hundreds of unwanted labourers. He resettled them at Juyongguan in Changping County of what is now Hebei Province — the name Juyong believed to be a shortened version of "Xi Ju Yong Tu", meaning "to resettle redundant people".

But Juyong has an important strategic place in history too. Flanked by high mountains and straddling a 20 kilometre long gully, it was regarded as a vital linchpin in the defence of northern China, and apparently so indo-mitable that it was the subject of at least one poetic tribute: "With only one soldier to defend the place, even ten thousand attackers will fail to capture it."

Near Juyong there is a terrace called Yuntai (Cloud Terrace) built in 1345 of white marble. It once supported three Buddhist stupas which were destroyed around the time of the late Yuan (Mongol) dynasty. A nearby monastery, Taian, built in 1439, was burned down in 1702. That which is left of Yuntai, the base, features an arched gate seven metres high and wide enough for a carriage to be driven through. The facade is decorated with Buddhist images which were carved there in the Ming reign. ▽△

Bada Range

The Bada Range (Eight-Reaching Pass) section of the Great Wall climbs high up a mountain range in the Yanqing area of Hebei, and offers one of the best surviving examples of the wall's defensive architecture and fortification. This area of the wall and its garrison were built in 1505 in the reign of the Ming emperor, Xiaozong, and they were definitely built to last. The wall itself is higher than most other sections, rests on huge stone slabs and is constructed almost entirely of brick and stone. The parapets are crenellated and the lower sections of the walls have loopholes for defensive fire by archers. The top surface of the wall is five metres wide, with space enough for five horses or 10 soldiers to march abreast along it.   △

Shanhaiguan

Shanhaiguan is a strategic garrison, built by the Ming general Xu Da in 1381, that lies at the far eastern end of the Great Wall, overlooking the Bo Sea. It is a powerful fortification, and rightly so, for it was regarded as the key to the capital itself. Aside from defensive walls, watchtowers and a central bell tower, the garrison features a two-storey "arrow tower" for archers and some 68 loopholes along its south, east and north walls through which a constant hail of arrows could be directed at attacking forces. When not in use these "arrow windows" were closed with red wooden shutters which had white discs and bull's eyes painted rather provocatively on them. With the Bo Sea to the south and the Great Wall snaking high into the adjacent mountains of the north — beginning its long march to the deserts of the west — Shanhaiguan is one of the most dramatic points along the 6,000 kilometre fortification. As an old poem describes it:

"I have heard of the great Shanhaiguan, But only today are my eyes truly widened. Ten thousand hectares of waves, one never tires of watching — Countless peaks and ravines, they are impossible to cross."   ▷

Ruins of the ancient city of Jiao He, in Xinjiang Province

The Western Region

The Western Region of China is an area of striking and somewhat bizarre physical contrasts. It is arid, yet rich in life-giving water resources. It covers vast areas of land that is flat, inhospitable and rated among the bleakest of the world's deserts — yet it also features massive snow-capped mountain ranges that roll like huge ocean waves into the Himalayas. It is an area of primary resources — minerals, salt, oil, chemicals and forest products — yet it is also the main setting for China's most advanced technology: its nuclear and aerospace centres. It has always been regarded as the main defensive frontier of Chinese civilisation, yet it was once the Middle Kingdom's only channel of communication with Central Asia, the Middle East and the rest of the world.

It is an area of some four million square kilometres embracing the Xinjiang-Uygur Autonomous Region, Gansu, Qinghai and Tibet (Xizang). In the north it borders the (Outer) Mongolian People's Republic, to the west, the USSR, and Jammu and Kashmir in northeast India; and to the south, Nepal, Bhutan and Burma. It features the highest river in the world, the Yalong and one of the world's highest lakes, the Namu, which lies north of the Tibetan capital, Lhasa.

The Xinjiang-Uygur Autonomous Region is divided by the Tian Mountains into two vast desert basins, the Tarim in the south and Junggar in the north. In the Tarim there lies one of the two most dreaded deserts in China, the Taklimakan, an 800,000 square kilometre stretch of 100 metre-high shifting dunes and fierce sandstorms. North of these basins lies the second most notorious desert waste, the Gobi, stretching northeast into Mongolia. In the southwest Xinjiang region it is a waterless sea of dunes and so inhospitable that local people call it the "land of death". In the central western Xinjiang the desert surface plunges more than 150 metres below sea-level to form the Turfan Depression, one of the lowest land surfaces on earth.

Despite its hostile terrain much of Xinjiang is also a vast underground freshwater cistern. Glaciers and melting snow from the region's four main mountain ranges, the Cong Range in the west, Altay in the northeast and Kunlun and Altun to the south, contribute to rivers that flow intermittently and frequently dry up,

and, more importantly, to immense underground reservoirs that feed surface springs, man-made wells and irrigation systems in surprisingly lush oases that dot the sands. These springs and wells have enabled no less than 13 minority groups in all, notably the Uygur, Kazakh, Huizu and tens of thousands of Han Chinese settlers to carve a solid foothold on the land.

The same water cycle saved many a trading caravan from perishing along another notorious stretch of the Silk Road. This mighty canyon, beginning in Wushao Range in the east and carving its way through the land to Yumen Pass at the western extremity of the Great Wall, was one of Central China's main thoroughfares to Central Asia and a natural entry point for armies of marauding Mongols. Because of its strategic importance it came under imperial attention, military and economic development from as early as the Han dynasty (206 BC-AD 220). The Great Wall itself is a prime military example.

Gansu also marks the point where the three tablelands of Mongolia, the loess (sandstone) area and Tibet converge. The great Yellow River rises in Tibet and cuts through the south of Gansu creating the spectacular Liujia and Sangyuan Gorges. Along with the Yellow River, the mightly Yangtze, Lancang and Nu Rivers of China begin there, and so do the sacred Ganges and Indus of India. The melting snows also feed more than 1,500 lakes throughout the Ngari and Nanqu regions of northern Tibet and in the high trans-Himalayan valleys of the south, it also forms China's greatest lake, Qinghai Lake, in the northeastern corner of Qinghai Province.

Qinghai is well endowed with rivers, providing fine pastureland in the southeastern areas, rich agricultural land along the Hehuang Valley and wheatlands. Xining, the capital, is the gateway to the Qinghai-Tibet Plateau. From here the landscape mounts in huge peaked steps to the "roof of the world", lifting into five great mountain ranges — Kunlun, Karakorum, Tanggula, Gangdise and Nyainqentanglha — that culminate in the Himalayas.

Although it is now under direct Chinese rule, Tibet was for centuries an independent state with a rigid politico-religious form of government in which authority was invested in the supreme head of the country's Buddhist faith, the Dalai Lama. Communication between the Tibetans and the Han Chinese goes back to the Tang dynasty (AD 618-907).

Mount Tomur

Towering more than 7,400 metres high, Mount Tomur is the highest peak of the Tian Range, a 2,800 kilometre wall of mountains that separates the arid Tarim and Junggar Basins in Xinjiang and stretches northwest into Soviet Central Asia. Called "Steel Mountain" by the local Uygur minority, Tomur is surrounded by 19 other peaks, all more than 6,000 metres high and snow-capped all the year round. More than 400 glaciers inch their way year by year through valleys and crevices, adding to the fairyland splendour of huge formations of ice — glistening towers and crags, frozen cascades, tunnels, caves, walls and bridges, and, here and there, even more fantastic natural art such as large boulders from the glacier faces supported on pillars of ice to form giant "mushrooms".

▷

The Snow Lotus

The Snow Lotus is one of very few plants that manage to flourish in a combination of thin air, bitter cold and increased ultra-violet light above the snow-line of the Tian Mountain Range. It can be found in sheltered spots on the slopes 3,000 to 4,000 metres high, an occasional burst of white petals with a slight yellow tint to them. Its stem is smooth and its roots are long, spreading deep into whatever earth it can find in the fissures and scars of the rocks in search of moisture and nourishment. Herbal pharmacists sell dried Snow Lotuses to mountain tribespeople, who soak them in spirits to prepare a concoction which they say cures backache, rheumatism and arthritis. ◁

Little Sky Lake (Xiaotianchi)

East of the Mount Tomur area, Mount Bogda rises nearly 6,000 metres, snow-covered and known locally as "Snow Sea". Nearby, its majestic slopes are mirrored in the waters of Little Sky Lake, a miniature lake covering about 50 square metres and surrounded by dense stands of fir and other trees.　△

The Tian Mountain Range

According to the Xiongnu people of the Xinjiang region — descendants of an ancient group of slave-owning nomad tribes — the Tian Range of mountains is "heaven". They also call them "White Mountains" or "Snow Mountains" and venerate them as their earth mother. Centuries ago, in the Han dynasty, the range was called the North Mountain, standing sentinel on the northwestern frontier of the infant Chinese nation-state against the marauding Xiongnu themselves.

The range rises in central Xinjiang and marches about 2,500 kilometres northwest into the heart of Soviet Central Asia. In Xinjiang it separates the Tarim and Junggar Basins, effectively dividing the autonomous region into northern and southern zones, and its lofty and precipitous path runs through other valleys and basins such as the Turfan Depression, Hami, Yanqi and Ili. At its eastern perimeter there are strategic mountain passes, notably the Seven-Cornered Well Pass and Dabancheng Pass, which have served for centuries as vital Central Asian gateways to China.

Most of the Tian Range's peaks are 3,000 to 5,000 metres high with Mount Tomur (7,435 metres) and Mount Hantengri (6,995 metres) dominating the range in the west, and Mount Bogda (5,445 metres) the highest in the east. The peaks are perennially snow-bound, and there are an estimated 6,896 glaciers in the range — an enormous reservoir of ice which, as it melts at the lower altitudes, becomes the fountainhead of rivers such as the Urumqi, Manas, Jing, Ili, Kaidu and Aksu. On the range's northern slopes there are grasslands and several varieties of hardy, high-altitude plants. Elsewhere, the slopes are rich in medicinal herbs, wildlife and minerals.

◁

Sky Lake in Tian Mountains

Not to be confused with Sky Lake in China's northeast, this smaller oblong lake, only three kilometres long, lies on the slope of Mount Bogda just under 2,000 metres above sea-level. It was referred to in a Ming dynasty novel as the place where the Taoist Heavenly Queen Mother held her birthday party. It was named Sky Lake in 1783 when the governor of Xinjiang laid a stone monument inscribed with the characters "heavenly mirror" and "godly pond".

Sky Lake was formed when debris from a glacier blocked a section of one of the rivers that carry melted snow from the upper slopes of Mount Bogda. The lake and its environs have become a popular holiday resort — a comfortable 15°C in summer and a relatively warm ice-skating centre in winter, even when the temperature on the northern slopes of Tian Mountains plunges as low as minus 40°C. The area around the lake is heavily wooded and contains a variety of valuable medicinal herbs. There are many scenic views and several Tibetan-style monasteries, notably Fushou Monastery, also called

White Poplar Gully (Baiyanggou)

Situated 60 kilometres south of Urumqi in Xingiang, White Poplar Gully is a summer resort made famous by its narrow waterway flanked on both sides by tall stands of poplars. It is also a natural pasture and a traditional gathering place for one of the region's main minority groups, the Kazakhs. Xinjiang has more minorities within its borders than any other political region of China. Alongside the Kazakhs in Xinjiang there are ethnic Russians, Tartars, Uzbeks, Tajiks, Xibes, Dours, Khalkhas, Mongols, Hui and a predominant population of Moslem Uygurs — a huge melting pot of many of the previously nomadic and obscure tribal groups of Central Asia.

At White Poplar Gully, visitors can watch the Kazakhs tending their sheep, horses and cattle, and may be invited to spend a night in their yurts. ▽

"Iron-Tiled Monastery" for its blue bricks and the grey, metallic colour of its tiles. △

63

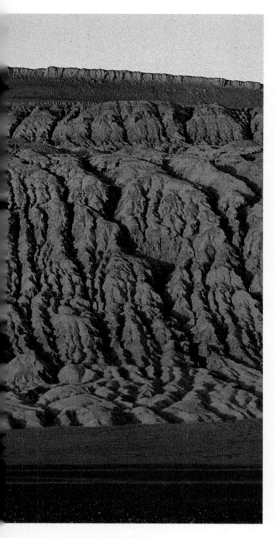

Flaming Mountains (Huoyan Shan)

A vivid example of the intense heat of the desolate Turfan Depression in Xinjiang is found in the Flaming Mountains in the north-central area of the basin, where the daytime temperature often reaches 70°C and an egg can be fried on the scorching rock of the slopes. When the sun strikes the rock and red soil the whole mountain range shimmers with the colours of fire, and deep vertical fissures in the slopes give the impression of tongues of flame licking the skies.

The mountains stretch east to west for about 100 kilometres across the Turfan Basin. ◁

Sugong Tower

Dominating the southeastern skyline of Turfan City, this Buddhist monument, erected in 1778, is 40 metres high and constructed of yellow bricks in 15 different patterns, each forming a decorative band around the walls. It has no foundation stones and is supported instead by a central spiral brick pillar with steps leading up to a viewpoint at the top. Next to the tower is a building that is equally imposing — a monastery built to accommodate more than 1,000 monks, students and worshippers. ▽

Lake Lop Nor

Over the past 2,000 years the lower Tarim River in Xinjiang has changed its course three times, depending on the amount of snow-fed waters feeding into it. And as the river has changed, so too has the position of Lake Lop Nor, the largest of China's salt water lakes. The current location of this vast salt-bed, surrounded by sand-dunes and salt crusts, is on the eastern edge of the basin bounded by the cities of Kuruktag, Yumen and Yangguan and Tikanlik.

But Lop Nor is really only a lake when the waters are available. Though its eastern extremity is submerged, forming many small lakes and marshes, it is generally regarded as simply a salt-covered lowland stretching over an area of about 3,000 square kilometres. It was an important landmark during the heyday of the Silk Road, and there are many historic temples, shrines and resting places on its shores. West of the lake is the site of an ancient trading centre, Loulan. Fierce winds from the Central Asian steppes ravage the lake's northeastern extremities, whipping up huge dunes of salt and then carving them into spectacular pillars. ◁

Ruins of Jiaohe

The dust-dry climate of the Turfan Depression has helped preserve more than one important historical relic, and notable among them are the ruins of a Uygur tribal city at Jiaohe, west of Turfan County. Constructed in the Tang dynasty of mud-brick and rammed earth, enough of the main structure stands today to give a clear picture of the thoroughfares and lanes, official halls, monasteries and pagodas, homes and courtyards, corridors and underground passages and thick earthen defensive walls of what was, in fact, a relatively sophisticated settlement. Underground chambers were dug below each dwelling to give shelter from the fierce daytime heat.

The ruins stand at the junction of two riverbeds and are overshadowed by a 30 metre high sheer cliff, the edge of a plateau, which was obviously an effective barrier against invasion. The town was abandoned in the latter part of the Ming dynasty, perhaps as a result of Han military pressure on the northern remnants of the preceding Mongol rule.

Ruins of Gaochang

Gaochang, another mud-brick ruin to the east of Turfan County, was once the capital of the state of Ouigour and an important way-station on the Silk Route. It stood as a strategic political, economic and cultural centre of the western frontier until the Ming dynasty when, like the settlement at Jiaohe, it was abandoned. From what is left of it today, it is obvious that it played an important military role on the frontier — it is surrounded by two defensive walls, the outer one standing from four metres to 11 metres high and 12 metres thick in some places. The remains of a huge monastery can be seen at the southwest corner of the wall, close to ruin of a tower that stood 15 metres high. ◁ △

The Beziklik Grottoes

The vitality with which Buddhism flowed through this, the Central Asian gateway to inner China, can be appreciated in the dramatic Beziklik Grottoes which lie on the slopes of a range of hills about 50 kilometres northeast of Turfan. They were probably built during the early flowering of the religion in China, in the time of the divided North and South dynasties of AD 420-589 before the rise of the powerful Tangs. Among the 64 grottoes that were either cut into the hillside or built of mud-brick and rammed earth, there are Buddha shrines and places of worship and cells which provided meditation retreats for the monks.

But the main feature of this sacred complex is the murals that adorn the walls of many of the chambers, most of them in poor condition but a great many that have withstood the ravages of time. They depict standing Buddhas, Bodhisattvas in the state of Nirvana, musicians, Buddhist and local folklore and, in one particular grotto, a dilapidated painting which is believed to be the only cave-mural in China dealing with Judgement and Hell. ▽

Uygur Tomb

The strong Islamic influence throughout China's western region — an influence going back to the Mongol Yuan dynasty's links with the Moslem empire — can be seen in the stunning architecture of the 17th century Uygur Tomb on the outskirts of Kashi in Xinjiang. It began as a family mausoleum, and today it presents a striking contrast of rustic simplicity and the ornate architecture of Islam — the eastern colours of its cone-shaped graves adding splendour to the principal grave chamber, a beautiful domed tomb decorated with green and amber tiles with minaret-style towers on all four corners. This main tomb contains 72 graves, most of them decorated with mosaic tiles and draped with colourfully patterned shrouds. One of them, as legend has it, contains the costumes of Xiangfei ("Fragrant Concubine"), a famous beauty who was kidnapped and installed in the Qing imperial court. ◁ ▽

Crescent Moon Spring (Yueyaquan)

This desert oasis lies among towering sand-dunes seven kilometres south of Dunhuang, and is said to be the place where the Emperor Wu of the Han dynasty found the coveted "blood-sweating" Wusun horses with which he was able to defeat and subdue the tribes of the western frontier. It is a small spring, only 100 metres long and 25 metres wide, but is fed so abundantly with subterranean water that it has never been known to dry up, even in the fiercest sandstorms. As the *Dunhuang County Gazette* describes it: "It is beautiful and unfathomably deep (and) remains clear, though threatened sometimes by tumultuous conditions of the surrounding dunes."

Rushes grow around the water's edge and there are trees on the east bank. In the spring the small lake becomes a popular visiting spot, especially at the time of the Duanwu Festival when pilgrimages are made to the nearby Mingsha Hill. The spring is also noted for one of its inhabitants, the "iron-back" fish, and a herb called "seven star", both of which have health-giving properties and have given the lake itself the name "Medicinal Spring". △

The Mogao Grottoes

Some of the greatest of China's Buddhist art treasures are found in the Mogao Grottoes, or "Thousand Buddha Caves", cut into the precipitous eastern slope of Mingsha Mountain about 25 kilometres southeast of Dunhuang. The earliest grotto was built in AD 366 by the monk Lochuan, and more than a thousand others were added in the following centuries. By the year AD 698 the complex was already so well established that Li Huairang produced an account called "Renovating the Buddhist Shrines in Mogao Grottoes".

Today only 492 grottoes remain, but they are packed with treasures — murals covering a total area of 45,000 square metres, 3,400 bas-relief and three-dimensional wall sculptures, several thousand pillars with the lotus motif and floral floor tiles and five ornate wooden shrines built in the Tang dynasty. In 1900 a Taoist priest named Wang Yuanlo opened up a sealed grotto and found some 50,000 Buddhist relics dating from the Jin to Song dynasties — scriptural texts, portraits, books, embroideries and much else.

The sculptural figures in the various caves are made of clay and painted, and they range in height from a few centimetres to 33 metres. The murals present a wide and colourful range of subjects, including gloomy and mysterious stories of the 5th to 7th centuries, exuberant and more refined paintings of the Buddhist scriptures from the period after the Sui dynasty (AD 581-618) and two particular murals showing an ancient map of Wutai Mountain and the "journey of Zhan Yichao and his wife". Pictured opposite is another remarkable grotto treasure, a huge sculpture of the Maitreya Buddha.

Polychrome Sculpture of Dunhuang

Clay was used for the wall-sculptures of the Mogao Grottoes, either in Yingsu, or bas-relief, or the three-dimensional Yuansu technique in which the work is detached completely from the wall. They represent different artistic styles from three separate historical periods.

Those sculptures from the first period, dating from the Northern Wei (AD 386-534), largely depict musicians attending to the Buddha, with characteristics that include straight high noses, long brows, large eyes, broad shoulders and flat chests and loose or diaphanous garments. The Bodhisattvas of this period are all male.

In the middle period, dating from the Sui to Tang Dynasties, the Sui sculptures feature large heads, robust physiques and disproportionately short legs, while those of the Tang era reflect the high standards of beauty and embellishment of the art of that time.

The last period, or school of Buddhist art, found among the Mogao treasures is that of the period of the Five Dynasties (AD 907-960) right through to the final imperial reign of the Qings.

The Wine Fountain (Jiuquan)

Like the Great Wall of China, the Wine Fountain, situated in a park of the same name in the Hexi Corridor of Gansu Province, reflects the abiding fear of invasion from the north. Throughout the Han dynasty, a confederation of slave-owning nomad tribes called the Xiongnu constantly harrassed the frontier. It is recorded that when the Han general Huo Qubing defeated the Xiongnu in a punitive war, Emperor Wu commanded that a large cask of wine be awarded to him for celebration. General Huo, wishing to share the wine with his soldiers, poured it into a spring and they all drank it from there. According to inscriptions on a stele that now stands nearby, the local villagers also found that the waters tasted like wine, and so gave the spring its name.

The Wine Fountain is fed by underground waters that flow by way of the Beida and Hongshui Rivers from the snows of Qilian Mountain. Its waters are crystal clear and do not freeze over in winter and were a vital life-saving landmark on this, one of the harshest sections of the Silk Route. A lake lies not far from the spring, fringed with white willows and tamarisks and beautified with a small bridge, an ornamental "zigzag" pathway and three pavilions. ◁ ▽

Wen Temple of Wuwei

The Wen Temple complex in Wuwei County, Gansu was built in 1437 and has since been renovated several times. The complex is 170 metres long and 90 metres wide, occupying an area of 153,000 square metres. One of the last major rebuilding projects took place during the reign of the Qing emperor Shunzhi.

There are two symmetrically arranged sections to the temple: two shrine halls on the east and Dacheng Hall, pictured above, on the west. Standing on a high brick and concrete platform, the hall features a double-eaved, half-hipped and half-gabled roof supported by cantilever brackets.

A stele now erected in the temple is the largest and the best-preserved stele with inscriptions in ancient Xixia script. It is 2.6 metres high, one metre wide and 30 centimetres thick. On the front, in Xixia script inscribed in the year 1094, is a detailed account of the reconstruction of a pagoda which was ruined by an earthquake and on the back is a translation in the Han language. △

White Horse Monastery (Baimasi), Qinghai

The horse is said to have originated in either Africa or Central Asia. But whatever its birthplace, its Asian contemporary, the Mongolian pony, has been valued and revered for centuries by the Chinese and their nomadic northern neighbours for its strength and endurance and military qualities. It is also one of the Seven Treasures of Chinese Buddhism, and is paid due respect by the Buddhists of Tibet and Qinghai Province at the White Horse Monastery, built into the lower slope of

Qinghai Lake

With no less than 50 rivers and streams flowing into Qinghai Lake it is not surprising that it is rated the largest inland body of water in China. Its surface covers an area of 4,600 square kilometres, and it lies 3,200 metres above sea-level. Around its shores are vast marshes and grasslands which the local inhabitants, mainly Tibetans, regard as especially fine pasture for sheep and cattle. A Tibetan community inhabits one of five islands in the lake, Haixin Hill, a granite outcrop that rises 76 metres above the water. It is a sacred spot and includes a temple. Another island, Bird Island (Niaodao), in the western reaches of the lake is a haven for migratory birds such as spotted wild ducks. Thousands of them flock to the island and the food-rich marshes around the lake in March and April, to be joined by huge flocks of "fish gulls", brown-headed gulls, cormorants and swans.　▽

a towering cliff to the east of Qinghai's capital, Xining.

The horse is also included in the pharmacopeia of Chinese medicine, with the pure white breeds said to have the most powerful medicinal qualities. In the *Ben Cao*, or Chinese *Materia Medica,* published in 1596, it says: "The heart, when dried and powdered and taken with wine, is a certain cure for forgetfulness . . . Above the knees the horse has night-eyes (warts) which enable him to travel in the night; they are useful in the toothache. If a man be hysterical when he wishes to sleep . let the ashes of a skull be mingled with water and given him, and let him have a skull for a pillow and it will cure him."　◁ △

Great Sutra Hall (Dajingtang)

The Great Sutra Hall is the Taer Monastery's principal building (opposite, bottom), a typical flat-roofed Tibetan structure erected in 1606. It was destroyed by fire in 1913 and rebuilt four years later with a total of 168 columns, some of them set into the walls, decorated with ornate carvings or hung with coloured rugs and embroidered pennants and streamers. The hall features a main theatre with prayer mattresses for 2,000 lamas. The walls are packed with volumes of the sutras and more than 1,000 gilded copper Buddha images. All in all, the Taer Monastery includes the Great Gold Tile Monastery, Little Gold Tile Monastery, Little Flower Monastery, Great Sutra Hall, shrine halls and a series of kitchens and dormitories. ▽

Taer Monastery

The Taer Monastery on the slope of Lotus Blossom Hill (Lianhua) in Huangzhong County is one of the largest lamaseries in Qinghai. It is also one of the most splendid examples of Tibetan Buddhist architecture and decor in the whole of the north and northwest. It was built in 1560 in memory of the founder of the Yellow Sect of lamaism, Tsongkhapa, and has been renovated and expanded several times since. It now comes under the Tibetan *Gong Bem* classification, meaning "a hundred-thousand Buddha images" for the many carved brick Buddha images of the chorten, or stupa, that dominates the centre of the complex.

As with most lamaseries in China, there are latter-day Han as well as traditional Tibetan influences here and there in the design. The main shrine hall (opposite page, top) is a Han-style structure with a triple-eaved, half-hipped and half-gabled roof and walls decorated with bright green glazed tiles. In 1711 the roof was retiled in gilded copper, thanks to a donation by a Mongol prince. A silver chorten dedicated to Tsongkhapa stands in the centre of the hall draped with yellow banners. The ceiling is a large mural of Buddhist scriptural tales, and the four walls are lined with several hundred volumes of the sutras. △

White Pagoda Hill (Baita Shan)

Rising to the north of Lanzhou City in Gansu, this hill is named after the White Pagoda on its peak — a 500-year-old structure that a series of violent earthquakes over the centuries has failed to destroy. The pagoda was built during the reign of the Ming emperor Jingzong (1450-1456) and stands within a terraced Buddhist complex that includes three shrine halls and two monasteries. Its position commands a view of the Yellow River and the entire city of Lanzhou. The hill itself rises from the north bank of the river to an altitude of 1,700 metres. On the slope below the pagoda lie two strategic garrison gates, Jincheng (Golden City) and Yudie (Jade Heap). ▽

Qilian Mountains

The Qilian Mountain Range extends more than 1,000 kilometres between Qinghai and Gansu Provinces, a series of parallel mountain walls that include the Tulai, Lenglong Range, Datong, and South Tulai Mountains. The highest peak, soaring to 5,800 metres, is in the South Tulai Range and the average height of the others is about 4,500 metres. The whole range is snow-capped, includes more than 3,300 glaciers and is the main source of water for the areas west of the Yellow River. The wide valleys are crisscrossed with streams and there are many lakes, the largest being Qinghai and Har.

At their lower levels the Qilian Mountains are heavily forested with firs and cedars, and the gentler slopes provide good pasture for sheep, cattle and horses. The mountains were once a stronghold of the Xiongnu alliance of tribes. When they were conquered and pushed out of the hills by the Han general Huo Qubing, a poem lamented their defeat.

"Having lost our Qilian Mountain, we have nowhere to breed our animals. Deprived of our Yanzhi* Mountain, our women are losing their true colours."

*Yanzhi can also mean "rouge" △

82

Jingang Hall

On his way to the war against the Xiongnu, General Huo Qubing is said to have bivouacked his troops at what is now known as Five Springs Hill in the southern district of Lanzhou in Gansu Province. His troops were thirsty, and there was no water to be found. The general, according to the story, pulled his sword and struck a rock. Water gushed from it, and so Five Springs Hill entered the vast realm of Chinese folklore.

Since then the hill and its springs have become an important Buddhist centre. The Chongqing, Mani and Kitigarbha Monasteries now stand there alongside the Sanjiao and Thousand Buddha Caves and various terraces and pavilions. Many of the original buildings were destroyed by border warfare against the Xiongnu "Huns" but the complex was restored in the reign of the Qing emperor Tongzhi in the years after 1868. The Jingang shrine hall is the oldest structure, erected in 1372 in the reign of Emperor Taizu of the Ming dynasty, and is the principal hall of the Chongqing Monastery. ▽

Bingling Monastery Grottoes

Excavated by Buddhist monks and converts in AD 420, the Bingling Grottoes on the northern bank of the Yellow River in Gansu's Yongjing County were developed over the centuries until there were 195 of them, packed with art and relics, by the time of the 13th century Mongol Yuan dynasty. Now, only 34 remain, but they contain nearly 700 carved stone Buddha images, more than 80 clay figures and 900 square metres of murals. There is also a stone pagoda and four others modelled in clay. The Buddha niches in the various caves are of the Indian style of Buddhist art and are rare in China. An inscription tells of the first work on the grottoes more than 1,500 years ago, and is the oldest cave writing in China.

The grottoes are cut into the western cliff-face of Dasi Gully, four rows of them extending more than two kilometres along the rock. Most of them date back to the Tang dynasty but many of the murals, though painted in the time of the Western Qin and Tang, were repainted during the Yuan dynasty of the Mongols. ▷

Sisters Peaks (Jiemeifeng)

Not far from Bingling Monastery stand two tall, straight peaks that look somewhat like two girls in the act of greeting acquaintances. Around them stand other strangely shaped rock formations, all of them of red sandstone. There are naturally many legends as to how they came to form that way, but the scientific reason is simply erosion. For many millions of years the sandstone was buried in soft loess soil. Over many more eons, the notorious annual floods of the Yellow River slowly ate the loess away to leave the sandstone exposed as outcrops, many of them as weirdly shaped as the so-called Sisters Peaks. ◁

Maiji Mountain

Lying southeast of Tianshui County in Gansu, Maiji is one of the hills at the western edge of the Qin Range. It is also the site of an inestimable wealth of buried treasure. In the years AD 384-417, hundreds of Buddhist grottoes were cut into the side of the hill. In AD 734, during the reign of Tang emperor Xuanzong, part of the cliff-face collapsed in a violent earthquake, burying many of the caves and the images, murals and other Buddhist artwork within them.

In 1941 a team of Chinese historians made the first serious study of the Maiji grottoes, and in 1952 a party of archeologists, accompanied by artists and photographers, carried out another survey to see if the sealed sections could be excavated. They found, however, that the cliff-face was too precipitous and dangerous — the cliff leans outward about eight metres at its peak — and so the treasures inside have remained buried.

In the 194 grottoes that survived the earthquake, more than 7,000 clay and stone sculptures and 1,300 square metres of murals have been found. The largest clay images are more than 15 metres tall. Of the murals, one of the most elaborate and interesting is that of a horse, pulling a carriage, which appears to change the direction of its walk as the viewer changes position. △

Mapam Yumco

Mapam Yumco, meaning "Unsurpassed Lake" in Tibetan, lies close to the sacred Kangrinboqe Peak in southwestern Tibet near the border with Nepal. According to some Tibetan records, the lake is actually the Yaochi, or Emerald Pond, where the Chinese Heavenly Mother of the West resides.

▽

Trashilungpo Monastery

One of the most interesting and historic Buddhist institutions in Tibet, the Trashilungpo Monastery, was erected by Gedun Truppa, the first Dalai Lama. It serves also as the tomb of the fourth Panchen Lama, and has been a religious and political centre since his death. Among its most treasured relics are volumes of the Buddhist canon written on palm leaves and elaborate silk tapestries of the Yuan and Ming dynasties. Situated southwest of Xin-gaze close to Tibet's southern border with Bhutan, the monastery covers an area of 20,000 square metres and comprises a palatial assembly hall and a scriptural hall, or theological college, along with numerous shrine halls — one of which houses a 26 metre-high bronze image of the Champa Buddha.

▷

Drepung Monastery

Drepung in Tibetan means "Large Heap of Rice" — not a very flattering comparison but one that manages to capture the white exterior decor and general design of this, one of the three greatest lamaseries of the Gelu, or Yellow Sect of Tibetan Buddhism. The monastery stands on a mountain slope about five kilometres west of the Tibetan capital, Lhasa. It was built in 1416 by command of the sect's founder, Tsongkhapa. The principal architecture is Tibetan and traditionally flat-roofed, but the main buildings incorporate Chinese-style gilded Buddhist wheels and other ornamentation.

The monastery is huge, accommodating 7,700 lamas and including different departments for education, ceremony and academic and general affairs. Its sutra hall alone is so enormous that between 8,000 and 9,000 lamas can pray and chant there at a time. ▷

Potala Palace

This massive fortified palace and monastery, the "Vatican" of Tibetan Buddhism, looms across the crest of the Red Hill to the northeast of Lhasa. Construction began in the 7th century when the Prince of Tubo, Songsten Gampo, built what was then known as the Red Roofed Palace in honour of his Chinese consort, Princess Wencheng. In 1642 the fifth Dalai Lama rebuilt the entire complex — pressing 7,000 slaves into what turned out to be a full 50 years of work — as the seat of Tibetan Buddhism and government. Since then Potala has comprised two main sections known as the Red and White Palaces, with the White Palace housing the Dalai Lamas and their vast courts of priests and monks and the Red Palace containing shrines, libraries and halls of worship. The buildings at the foot of the hill include administrative offices, workshops, a printing press and a prison.

As a palace-castle complex, Potala is as security-conscious as it is sacred. Walls of enormous granite blocks protect it, along with a number of fortresses. As an added precaution, the walls are said to be reinforced with copper to strengthen them against earthquakes.

The Sun Hall of the Potala

Despite its altitude and the bitter cold of winter, Lhasa is known as the Sun City of Tibet for the long hours of daylight that it enjoys, about twice that of any other place in the same latitude. For this reason the living quarters of the Dalai Lama were built on the top of the Potala, and named the Sun Hall. It's here that the supreme rulers spent their winter months in comfortable and ornate surroundings.

It is these living quarters that the Chinese Government has recently renovated, possibly in anticipation (or hope) of the return to Lhasa of the present exiled Dalai Lama. Another reason for the preservation work could, however, be tourism. Thousands of visitors, most of them from the West, have filed through the Potala and the Sun Hall since Tibet was reopened to foreigners in 1980, here to view the magnificent apartment and such decor and relics as the wands, lined with tiger fur, that are the Dalai Lamas' symbol of absolute authority; the predominant red and gold decoration of the rooms and their many priceless tapestries, carpets, murals and sculptures of Buddhas and Bodhisattvas; the intricate carvings of the screens and furnishings and the vivid splashes of colour from the woven and embroidered pillar rugs.

All the gold and silver utensils used by successive Dalai Lamas are on display, along with teacups and bowls of carved jade, amber bowls and gold and silver goblets, and gold vases that weigh up to four kilograms a piece. The throne of the Dalai Lama stands on the north side of the hall, and beside it are placed a human-skin drum and a wine bowl made from a human skull — tokens of his power and influence. Though certainly bizarre to Westerners, the use of human bones in this fashion is, in fact, a venerated tradition of Tibetan Buddhism. In traditional death ceremonies, for example, corpses are left exposed on mountain slopes to be picked clean by animals and birds, then the bones are smashed and flung into ravines — symbolising the conviction that it is the spirit, travelling toward reincarnation, that is sacred; the worldly remains are of no importance at all.

Dragon King Pond

When the 5th Dalai Lama rebuilt and remodelled the Potala three centuries ago, the landscaping and the foundation work for the fortifications left a big hole in the ground on the palace's northern slope. This became the small lake, Dragon King Pond, which takes its name from a pavilion called Dragon Palace on an island in its centre. Tibetans gather at the pond each year to celebrate a legend which has emerged from the project. It is said that at one time a huge lake lay where the city of Lhasa now stands. A dragon came up out of the lake each year to demand the sacrifice of a young boy. On one occasion a boy named Dun Yue was selected. But instead of submitting meekly to his fate, Dun Yue challenged the dragon and, after a fierce battle lasting seven days and nights, finally slew it. From that moment on, the lake gradually receded and the area became dry land. ▽

The New Palace of Norbu Lingka

When not in residence in the Potala's Sun Hall, the Dalai Lamas ruled Tibet from Norbu Lingka, their summer villa. Shortly before the present Dalai Lama (14th reincarnation) fled to exile in northern India, he added the New Palace in the eastern part of the grounds, north of Dragon King Temple. A two-storey flat-roofed building in the traditional Tibetan design, its interior is lavishly decorated with murals illustrating Tibetan history and stories from the Buddhist scriptures. There is a prayer hall, also lined with murals and carpeted from wall to wall in dark red. The roof is embellished with gilded sculptures that include the Buddhist Wheel of Law flanked on both sides by a golden gazelle in a kneeling position, eyes turned to the wheel to symbolise devotion to the Buddhist faith. ▷

Norbu Lingka

Norbu Lingka itself is a white-walled villa complex which in Tibetan is called "Treasure Garden". It lies about one kilometre west of Potala Palace. The industrious 7th Dalai Lama, obviously following the tradition set by the Chinese emperors, built this seasonal retreat on what until then had been a grove of brambles. He designed it in three sections, the palace, monasteries and a well-laid park of ponds, pavilions and scenic pathways. His successor added a Mid-Lake Palace, built in the Chinese architectural style — a series of ornate buildings and pavilions resting on a podium two metres above the waters of the lake. With its traditional Chinese decor of dark jade-coloured tiles and red columns, the palace stands out most effectively against its wooded backdrop. ▽

Sela Monastery

Along with the Drepung and Gandan Monasteries, the Sela Lamasery in the northern district of Lhasa is one of the "Three Great Monasteries" of Tibetan Buddhism. It is also one of the six Gelu, or Yellow Sect lamaseries — its lamas wearing yellow caps to signify membership of this particular Buddhist following. The name "Sela" comes from the origins of the monastery: according to records the site on which it stands was a big orchard abundant with a citrus fruit called *se*. It is said that when Tsongkhapa, the father of the Yellow Sect, was riding through the grove his horse neighed three times — and he interpreted this as meaning

that in three years' time the Horse-Headed Heavenly Guard, a guardian spirit of Buddhism and a reincarnation of Avalokitesvara Buddha, would descend to earth. Tsongkhapa ordered that a shrine hall be erected on the spot.

Later, one of his disciples, Jamchen Choje, built the Sela Monastery itself, with the Horse-Headed god as its main deity. Other interesting Buddhist relics and treasures in the lamasery include a silver chorten containing the remains of a Dalai Lama and decorated with jewellery and precious stones, a Tibetan sutra written in gold and a set of sandalwood figures of the Buddhist deities brought from Beijing by the monastery's founder, Jamchen Choje.

The shrine hall, opposite, was the principal assembly hall of the monastery. Its dominant role and position in the arrangement of buildings distinguishes it from the others, opposite, top.

95

Mount K2 (Godwin Austen)

This mountain of the vast Karakoram Range, standing on the border of China and Kashmir in the southwest corner of Xinjiang, is 8,611 metres high and the second tallest peak on earth. Shaped something like a pyramid, it is also said to be steeper and more hazardous than the world's highest peak, Mount Everest. Terrific winds tear at its upper slopes creating avalanches which crash down on to the glaciers below, actually pushing at them and making them flow faster. The great height, extreme cold and strong radioactivity of the area were considered too hostile to human venture until 1954,

when two Italian mountaineers — supported by 500 local sherpas — succeeded in fighting their way to the summit.

The Kunlun Range extends from Pamir Plateau ("Roof of the World") to the southeast, to join the Himalaya Range — a distance of 500 kilometres. It is about 250 kilometres wide, the average height being 6,100 metres above sea level with 18 peaks of more than 7,600 metres above sea level. ◁

Mount Qomolangma

This, the mightiest mountain in the world at 8,848 metres, is called Everest by Westerners who see it as a supreme test of courage and endurance, and is regarded as the Goddess of the Snow Mountains by Tibetans, who venerate it for its beauty and grandeur. Over the centuries they have built palaces and gardens around its lower slopes — and a lamasery called Rongbu, which has the distinction of being the loftiest religious institution in the world.

Everest, or Qomolangma, is often shrouded by clouds and mist which the Tibetans say is the "veil of the Holy Mother". For Western expeditions, these swirling mists are one of Everest's terrors, along with hurricane-force winds and storms that suddenly lash the snow and ice-covered slopes, the bitter temperatures (normally between 30°C and 40°C below zero), the lack of oxygen on the upper precipices and the summit itself, which is little more than a precarious ridge about one metre wide and 12 metres long — a tiny pinhead at the very roof of the world.

On the Tibetan side of Qomolangma there are 217 glaciers and one vast stretch of the slopes, between 5,700 metres and 6,700 metres, which is literally a forest of ice. Its "trees" are huge columns and towers of frozen runoff. Beyond this, at 7,500 metres, it is so cold and bleak that much of Everest's face is simply craggy and precipitous bare rock. ◁△

The Silk Road

Chinese silk has been admired the world over since time immemorial, yet each bale of the precious material that ever reached the West had to make a perilous journey across thousands of miles of desert wastes and Central Asian steppes along that most romantic of all trade routes, the Silk Road.

A major expansion of China's silk trade with the West came about as a result of military endeavour. The Han dynasty emperor Wu, who reigned from 140-88 BC, sent envoys into what is now Soviet Uzbekistan in search of fabled "blood-sweating" horses, said to have descended from the heavens, to aid him in his wars against Xiongnu and Mongol incursions on the northern and western frontiers. His decision turned out to be a wise one, for in one campaign after another these sturdy, fleet-footed Mongol ponies pushed back the "Huns" until they were finally expelled from the entire Gansu region. This military success opened up the route that the first western-bound trading caravans took, setting out in 114 BC and soon followed by many others until 12 trading expeditions were pushing west through the deserts each year. Each caravan consisted of roughly a hundred merchants, emissaries and retainers, along with a train of camels each capable of carrying loads of up to 140 kilograms for up to 30 kilometres a day.

The name "Silk Road" was coined by the German scholar Ferdinand Von Richthofen. The trade route began in Xi'an and passed along the Hexi corridor to the oasis at Dunhuang and then on to Yumenguan (Jade Gate) at the westernmost point of the Great Wall. From there it divided into two routes, giving caravans a choice of going north or south of the dreaded Taklimakan Desert. The northern trail struck out across the desert toward Hami. Hugging the foothills of the Tian Range it passed through Turpan, Karashahr, Kucha, Aksu and Tumchuq to Kashi. The southern trail followed the fringes of the Tibetan plateau, travelling via the oases at Miran, Endere (Tuhoho), Niya (Minfeng), Keriya (Yutian), Khotan (Hotian) and Yarkant (So Che). From there it turned northward to rejoin the northern route at Kashgar.

From here the Silk Road continued westward and climbed the dangerous High Pamirs before passing out of Chinese territory into what is now Soviet Central Asia, continuing via Khokang, Samarkand, Bokhara and Merv through Persia and Iraq and on to the Mediterranean coast.

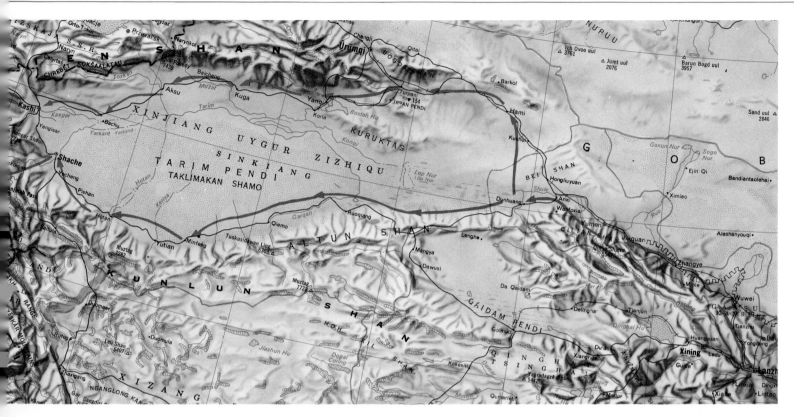

Xi'an's City Wall

The modern city of Xi'an, which lies to the southeast of Shaanxi Province, was known as Changan and served as the ancient Chinese capital from the time of the 11th century BC rule of the Western Chou to the triumph of the Tangs. From the 3rd century BC it was also a vital commercial centre because of its position on the eastern stretches of the Silk Route. Its trading importance and its vulnerability — lying in the path of the main Central Asian conduit into the heart of central China — also made it one of the most heavily fortified cities of the north.

From its earliest days, a defensive wall encircled it, and in 1374 in the large programme of defensive works undertaken by the Ming the city's present wall was built — a massive stone structure, strengthened with fortifications, running for about 12 kilometres around Xi'an, rising 12 metres high and spreading 14 to 18 metres thick at its base. They include some 98 watchtowers, nearly 6,000 crenels cut into a parapet that runs right around the top of the wall. There are four huge gates, over which the Ming dynasty engineers built small multi-storey forts with observation points and firing ports from which teams of archers and sappers could shower the attacking forces with arrows, gunpowder bombs and blazing oil and naphtha. ◁

Mingsha Hills

Six kilometres south of Dunhuang and close to the Crescent Moon oasis, the fierce winds of the desert have whipped the sands into a series of tall and dramatically shaped dunes called Mingsha Hills. Legend has also added to the drama of this strangely beautiful place. The name of the dunes translates as "Murmuring Sand", referring to a noise like distant thunder that comes from the action of the wind on the sail-like curves that it has sculptured in the dunes' faces. It is said that there was once a general who set up camp here on his way to the western frontier. In the night a violent sandstorm blew up and buried him along with his army. The "murmur" from the dunes is said to be the cries of the buried souls. △

Dafangpancheng

Windswept sun-baked ruins of mud-brick walls are all that are left of Dafangpancheng, a garrison built in the Han dynasty, roughly 2,000 years ago, between Dunhuang and Yumenguan in the Gobi Desert. The stronghold had considerable strategic value, standing close to the western terminal of the Great Wall and providing storage for provisions, equipment and fodder for the Han defenders based at other garrisons and watchtowers in the Yumenguan area. It also served as a way-station on the Silk Route. When traders began using another trail that ran across the northern area of Gansu Province, Dafangpancheng and other towns around it fell into decline. ▷

Jade Gate (Yumenguan)

In the Han era Yumenguan was a gateway to Central Asia and the principal market for jade from all over Xinjiang Province. But when the trade shifted away to the north the city fell into ruin, and since the Tang dynasty there has been much argument about where it actually stood. It was only recently, with the discovery of important Han dynasty documents in Dunhuang, that scholars were able to agree that ancient Jade Gate — not to be confused with modern Yumen Town and Yumen City — was located on what is now the site of Little Fangpancheng.

Yumenguan represented the boundary between civilised Han China and the dangerous barbarian lands of the western frontier. The autobiography of Ban Chao in the latter part of the Han dynasty speaks of the area as if it were the very edge of the world. "Your Majesty's subject," he wrote, "does not hope to come to the Wine Springs, but does wish to cross the Yumenguan while still alive." △

Ancient Altar (Gujitai)

Ten kilometres west of Turfan, a monolith of mud-brick and rammed earth rears up out of the boundless desolation, standing in tribute to the glory of the Silk Road, the Buddhist faith that took root along it, and those who survived the gruelling journeys to and from the West. This massive altar forms the centrepiece of the ruins of Jiaohe, a strategic Silk Road city during the Han and Tang dynasties. Jiaohe and nearby Gaochang were among dozens of cities and towns that sprang up along this section of the trade route, their populations ranging from a few hundred to as many as 10,000. When the busy overland route eventually succumbed to competition from the seas — a death knell that sounded during the great ocean trading expeditions of the Ming dynasty — these centres became ghost towns and were gradually engulfed by the desert sands. Around the Ancient Altar, the ruins of Jiaohe have weathered the centuries reasonably well, and it is still possible to trace the sites of public buildings, streets and defensive walls. ▽

Bogda Peak

Bogda Peak rises 5,445 metres out of the desert in Fukang County northeast of Urumqi to present a striking contrast of burning sands and frigid snow-capped summit. It is not the highest peak in the Tian Range — those of Mount Tomur and Mount Hantengri are more than 1,000 metres higher — but it has the advantage of being clearly visible from all points of the surrounding desert basins. To add to the contrast of heat and ice, its principal face has a gradient of 60 degrees, down which the snow crashes in huge avalanches, feeding more than 80 glaciers that lie in the gullies and crevices of its lower slopes. ▷

Ruins of Subashi

Not only cities and towns but splendid Buddhist monasteries crumbled into ruin when the Silk Road was overtaken by maritime transport as the main vehicle of the rich China trade. Only the jagged stumps of walls remain of the Subashi Monastery, 23 kilometres east of Kuqa County on the banks of the Tongchang River, but even these provide evidence of the lamasery's former splendour — the traces of three pagodas that overlooked the shrine halls and terraces. To the north of the ruins a row of grottoes lines the hillside, their walls featuring carved Buddha images and inscriptions in the Kuqa language. Many relics have been unearthed in the Subashi ruins, including bronze utensils, iron-ware, pottery, wood carvings, murals and clay sculptures. ▽

The Kizi Kuqa Beacon Tower

Standing 10 kilometres west of Kuqa County, this watchtower — or the weatherbeaten remains of it — was one of many built along the southern arm of the Silk Road to protect travelling merchants and emissaries from bandits. It also stood sentinel against the Xiongnu tribes which constantly probed and attacked the northern frontiers during the Han dynasty. The tower, constructed of rammed earth reinforced with timber and reeds, was linked to a regional office and a series of garrisons at Kuqa. In an emergency, observers put up flag and smoke signals to alert the forts. According to records found at Juyan and Dunhuang, six combinations of signals were used, involving flags, smoke and fire and drums. At the top of the ruin, wooden rafters can be seen jutting from the walls suggesting that it once had a reconnaissance balcony. ▽

Bostan Lake

The ancient south Tianshan route of the Silk Road stretches along the northeast to the west border of the lake, commanding a strategic position of the trade route.

Bostan in Mongolian means "Nomads like to stop here", and after a gruelling, dangerous and very thirsty struggle through the southern reaches of the Gobi Desert, Boston was paradise itself. Lying in the Yanqi Basin south of the Tian Mountain Range, the lake is about 55 kilometres long and 25 kilometres wide. With a 9.9 billion cubic metre capacity, it is the largest freshwater lake in Xinjiang. It lies in a high-level area, at an altitude of just over 1,000 metres, and is frozen over in winter. The lake takes its waters from three rivers that cut through the parched terrain and are fed in turn from the snows of the Tian Mountains.

Bostan Lake provides oases and irrigation along it banks for the cultivation of melons, apricots, plums, peaches, grapes and the famous and delectable Korla pears. Its waters are well stocked with many varieties of fish and it supports a large area of reeds and rushes, of which some 300,000 tonnes are harvested each year and used for the manufacture of paper, handicrafts, and building materials. Not far from its southeast bank there is a smaller saline lake which produces pure salt.   △

The Forbidden City, Beijing

The Central Region (North)

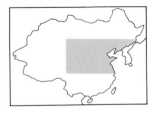

For thousands of years the north central region of China has been the cradle of Chinese civilisation and the nation's political powerhouse. Its Yellow River Basin is the site of one of the most important archeological discoveries of all time — the skull of "Peking Man", unearthed at Zhoukoudian in Hebei Province and regarded as evidence of human existence along the riverflats no less than half a million years ago. The region's major cities, such as Luoyang, Kaifeng, Xi'an and, of course, Beijing, have been the nation's seats of power, either dynastic strongholds or imperial capitals, at various times in the vast span of history from the early Warring States to the collapse of the Manchu Qings.

It is a region immensely rich not only in history but also natural resources. Its soil is largely soft loess and exceptionally fertile. It encompasses the world's greatest man-made waterway, with the waters of the mighty Yellow River, Hai River and Yangtze River linked and harnessed by the Grand Canal — itself a monumental waterway built over a period of more than 2,000 years between Hangzhou and Tianjin — to support vast croplands of wheat, cotton, corn, sorghum, peanuts, tobacco and soyabeans and to provide an efficient and relatively cheap inland transport system for agricultural products and the region's huge deposits of coal, iron ore and salt.

The region embraces the loess tableland south of the Great Wall and the Central China Plain, which covers the provinces of Shaanxi, Shanxi, Henan, Hebei and Shandong. While not as physically dramatic as its neighbouring regions to the northeast and northwest, it features two large mountain ranges, the Hua in the west, the central Song Range and a terrain that slopes to the east — the Yellow River tracing this gradual eastward descent as it cuts through the loess plateau and then curves through the Central Plain to empty into the Bo Sea. On its way the river deposits vast quantities of alluvial soil, a process which gave birth to agricultural settlement along its banks 5,000 to 6,000 years ago but has also given the river itself the name "China's Sorrow". In areas near its estuary the alluvial deposits are so heavy that the river's bed has risen many metres above the level of the surrounding land. Despite a complex system of dykes, established over the centuries to check and tame the river's course, occasional tremendous flooding has cost thousands upon thousands of lives.

The region also offers a history that is just as rich — its imperial cities, dominated by the majesty and grandeur of Beijing's Forbidden City, the home of 24 Chinese emperors; its temples, monasteries and other religious monuments, notably the magnificent Confucian Temple in Shandong, the Shao Lin Monastery in Song Shan and the many Buddhist temples and shrines in Heng Mountain; and its renowned archeological treasure house, the city of Xi'an, where, among other relics, the terra cotta army of the father of Chinese unity, the first Qin emperor, stands guard over the souls of China's imperial past.

Qingzhen Mosque

Xi'an (Western Peace) has a long and illustrious history going back to the Zhou dynasty of 1,122 BC, and as late as the turn of this century was the seat of the Qing imperial court when it retired there to avoid the excesses of the Boxer Rebellion. The city also has more mosques within its boundary than any other in China, one of the most interesting of which is the Qingzhen Monastery, built in 1392 with a main hall big enough to accommodate 1,000 worshippers.

▽

Qian Tombs

Magnificent stone lions guard the entrance to this, the burial place of Emperor Gaozong and Empress Wu of the Tang dynasty. The mausoleum, hewn out of three hills, lies at Liang Mountain in Qian County, Shaanxi. Besides the stone lions, ostriches, winged horses and soldiers that surround the tomb, there are statues of 61 leaders of regional ethnic minorities and foreign diplomats of that time. Emperor Gaozong died in AD 684, and his queen 22 years later. ◁

Chenghuang Temple

This Ming dynasty temple in Sanyuan County, Shaanxi, was constructed in 1375 and is now one of the country's best-preserved examples of Ming architecture — it has kept its original design ever since it was first built. Over the centuries it has been both a place of worship, where people pray for rain, good fortune or protection, and a meeting place for merchants. In its post-imperial role it has also served as a venue for the performing arts. ◁

Yellow Emperor Tomb (Huangdiling)

The Yellow Emperor is credited with being the father of traditional Chinese medicine, the inventor of agriculture and the father of the Chinese race itself. His tomb in Qiaoshan in Huangling County, Shaanxi, was built in the Song dynasty to replace an earlier monument set up in the time of the Han. At the foot of a hill close to the tomb there are 14 cedar trees, one of which is said in legend to have been planted by the Yellow Emperor himself. A large plaque in the main hall bears the inscription "First Ancestor of Humanity". △

Great Wild Goose Pagoda (Dayanta)

This magnificent pagoda south of Xi'an, was built by the Buddhist monk Tripitaka to store the sutras which he brought from India during the first flowering of the religion in China. The pagoda takes its name from a compelling incident, recorded in Tripitaka's biography, in which a flock of wild geese flew over a monastery in Magadha, a kingdom in Central India. One of them broke its wings and fell from the sky. The monks, believing that it was a Bodhisattva, buried it and built the pagoda in its honour.

The pagoda had only five storeys when it was first built, and two others were added in the time of the Five Dynasties. It bears inscriptions by the Tang emperors Taizong and Gaozong. During their reigns it was customary for successful candidates in the civil service examinations to be entertained at the nearby Apricot Garden and then taken to Great Wild Goose Pagoda for their signing ceremony. It became a great honour for scholars to "sign at the Great Wild Goose Pagoda", and the poet Bai Juyi went one step further than that. "Of those who signed beneath the Great Wild Goose Pagoda, seventeen in all," he wrote, "I was the youngest." △

Drum Tower of Xi'an

While Western medieval towns and forts had nightwatch sentries to call the hours of the night, a large drum on the upper floor of this two-storey tower in Xi'an boomed out the coming of darkness. The Drum Tower was built in 1380 in the reign of the Ming emperor Taizu and was renovated twice in the following centuries. It is remarkably well preserved, and is one of the historic showpieces of a city whose name is synonymous with Chinese history. ▷

Little Wild Goose Pagoda (Xiaoyanta)

Located in Jianfu monastery. close to the southern gate of Xi'an, the Little Wild Goose Pagoda has a most tumultuous history — it has been struck by no less than 70 earthquakes since it was first built in the year 707, and has survived every one of them. According to the city's records, one of the tremors in 1487 was so violent that it left a split a third of a metre wide right down the middle of the tower. But 34 years later it was struck again — and this time the action of the quake closed the crack again. But the pagoda hasn't survived completely unscathed. It was originally 15 storeys high, but earthquakes destroyed the two top floors.

In Jianfu Monastery there hangs a large bell that was cast and installed in the Ming dynasty. A beautiful poem pays tribute to its toll:

"Frost accompanies the greyish break of dawn
On which is painted the still dallying moon.
My dream is broken by the sound of the monastery bell
Which for ten centuries haunted the mystic air." ▷

Forest of Steles (Beilin)

In the Tang dynasty, when Xi'an was called Chang'an, the city was noted for its large collection of stone steles, many of them featuring fine examples of early Chinese calligraphy or carvings of the Thirteen Classics of Confucian philosophy. In the year AD 904 it was decided to bring the entire collection under one roof, so to speak, and a place was reserved within the city wall. But it took another 186 years for work to be completed on Xi'an's Forest of Steles, a sprawling complex of exhibition halls, covered corridors and a pavilion, which nowadays houses more than 1,000 steles and tomb-tablets.

The exhibition virtually encompasses the history of Chinese writing, presenting the calligraphy of the Qin dynasty of the third century BC, through the Tang and Song and into the Ming and final Qin reigns. In AD 1555 a powerful earthquake caused extensive damage to the halls, and the complex was rebuilt at the end of that century. Three new halls were added during the 17th and 18th centuries.

The impressive collection includes all the representative styles of Chinese

Tomb Pagoda of Tripitaka

The monk Tripitaka was one of the founding fathers of the Buddhist faith in China. He was entombed in AD 669 on the slope of Shaolingyuan in what is now Changan County, Shaanxi. A monastery and pagoda were built in his memory, and when Emperor Suzong visited the site he inscribed the characters "Xing Jiao" (Promotion of Religion) on a plaque, and that became the monastery's name.

A small chamber inside the five-storey 21 metre-high pagoda houses a sculpture of Tripitaka. Being a tomb, the upper storeys are filled with earth.

To each side of the tower there are smaller pagodas built as tombs for his principal disciples, Kuiji and Yuance. Tripitaka set out from China along the Silk Road in AD 629 on a journey in search of Buddhist scriptures from India. It took him four years to reach there. After another 16 years of study he returned to China with some 600 or more sutras, then spent another 19 years translating them into Chinese. In all, he contributed 1,335 volumes to the vast bibliography of Buddhist literature in China. ▽

calligraphy such as the ancient official script, the highly abstract cursive script, and the artistic writings of the great painter-poets, all of which became models for later students of calligraphy.

Some of the steles on display are of great historical value, such as the stele recording the introduction of Christianity into China. Another remarkable stele is a bas-relief called the "Six Steeds of Zhao Mausoleum". It is in fact the tombstone of Taizong, the second emperor of the Tang dynasty, and shows the six splendid war horses which he rode in campaigns against the northern "barbarians". ◁ △

The Pond of Glorious Purity (Huaqingchi)

One of the eight most celebrated places of natural beauty in central China, the Pond of Glorious Purity in Shaanxi Province is also the location of a hot springs system that is steeped in history and legend. The first Qin emperor is said to have built a travelling lodge beside the springs, which are found on the slope of Mount Li in the south of Lintong County. According to folklore, on one of his visits he encountered an Immortal disguised as a common peasant woman, who, taking exception to his rather familiar behaviour toward her, spat in his face. The

emperor's features immediately broke out in a dreadful skin ailment. Apologising profusely for his indiscretions, the emperor begged her to remove the curse — and the woman revealed herself as an Immortal and bathed his face in the spring, curing him as swiftly as he had been afflicted. Thereafter, the hot springs of Mount Li were known as the Immortal Hot Springs.

Another of the springs, called Hibiscus, became the trysting spot of the Tang emperor Xuanzong and his beautiful concubine Yang — the poet Bai Juyi, in his poem "Song of Everlasting Woe", describing how the "streams of the warm fountain / Caressed her waxen limbs".

Hua Mountain

Hua Mountain (Western Sacred Mountain), lying south of Huayin County in Shaanxi, is another dramatic beauty spot that for centuries has been a symbol of the Chinese reverence and delight in nature. The names alone that have been given to its various peaks and viewpoints bear tribute to a feeling that goes beyond mere popularity. Its name translates into Great Flower Mountain; its highest peak, Luoyan (2,200 metres), is Descending Wild Duck Peak. Another of its summits, Jade Girl (Yunu) Peak, commemorates the daughter of a Zhou dynasty prince who renounced her aristocracy to come to live on Hua Mountain with a flute player and recluse named Xiaoshi. Nearby, Gold Lock (Jinsuo) Pass leads to Lotus Blossom (Lianhua) Peak, and another path climbs to Facing Sun (Zhaoyang) Peak where there is a ter-race built for the viewing of the sunrise. East of Zhaoyang, Immortal's Palm Cliff celebrates a legend in which a river god called Juling created the course of the Yellow River, leaving a palm-print in the rock to remind mortal beings of the cataclysmic event.

Three Springs

In the Jin Shrine in Taiyuan City in Shanxi there are three springs, two of which flow intermittently and a third called Nanlao (Loath to Get Old) which gushes constantly and maintains the same 17°C temperature, all year round. A pagoda nearby called Water Mother Mansion refers to a legend which has also sprung from the bore. It appears that when Water Mother was a young maiden she had to fetch water over a long and tiring distance each day. A mysterious stranger gave her a whip and told her to store it in her water jar, and to take it out only when she wanted water. When her domineering mother-in-law saw that she was cheating on her chore, she confiscated the magic whip — and the jar has overflowed with water ever since.   ◁

Jin Shrine

Jin Shrine, a complex of 100 or so halls, shrines and pavilions, has a history so vast that the exact date of its construction is still a matter of conjecture. It is mentioned, however, in the classic *Shui Jing Zhu*, written more than 1,400 years ago, as being built in memory of Shuyu, the second son of Emperor Wu of Zhou (1122-1115 BC). It has been renovated several times since then. Set in a beautifully landscaped garden of trees and streams, it offers some of the most interesting and valuable examples of different dynastic architecture found anywhere in China, along with several clay images that are considered masterpieces of Chinese art.

△

Huayan Monastery

Construction of Huayan Monastery in southwest Datong, Shanxi, began in the Liao dynasty (AD 916-1125) and reflects the superstitions of the Khitan tribespeople who swept down from the north to seize China's central plain. The halls and shrines all face the east to conform with the Khitan worship of the sun and their fear of evil influences from other points of the compass. The monastery was renovated in the Ming period of the 15th century and divided into upper and lower terraces. The upper monastery, containing the principal hall, Daxiongbaodian, built in the Jin dynasty (1115-1234), features 31 clay sculptures of Liao period Bodhisattvas. ◁

The Great Hall (Daxiongbaodian)

The Great Hall of the Upper Temple of the Huayan complex was rebuilt in 1140, then renovated during the Ming reign — and has been given additional touches right up to the turn of this century. The murals of the main hall, 900 square metres of them, depict the life of Sakyamuni Buddha, images of arhats, thousand-eye Bodhisattvas and the fierce pantheon of Chinese gods that were painted in 1875 to 1908 by the artist Dong An. Among the many relics in the shrine hall are five gilded Maitreya Buddhas seated on lotus pedestals and more garish statues of 20 Heavenly Guards. ▽

Yungang Caves

The Yungang grottoes are located 16 kilometres west of Datong in Shanxi. Carved into the northern slope of Mount Wuzhou more than 1,500 years ago, they are rated as one of the three most significant examples of Buddhist cave art in China. Ancient records indicate that the caves were situated close to a community of Buddhist monasteries flourishing in the Liao and Jin periods. There are now 53 caves in all, covering almost one kilometre of the cliff face and containing over 51,000 Buddhist images. Three different periods and styles of Buddhist art are represented. Stupas of innumerable forms and variations are found in the eastern caves, while the western caves contain figures which bear the influence of Indian art. The central caves, the largest and earliest to be carved, contain images which are said to have been modelled on the rulers of the northern Wei dynasty of AD 386-534. Grottoes 16-20 each contain a statue of Buddha at least 13 metres tall. The one in grotto number 18 (below) is the most imposing, while the gigantic Buddha sitting outside grotto number 20, with a dignified but faintly amused expression, is said to be carved in typical northern Wei style.

Grotto Number 13

Grottoes numbers 9–13 at Yungang are known as the Wuhua Caves and are noted for the ornate and brightly coloured flower-and-plant motifs, altars, sculptured musicians and instruments added there by artists of the Qing dynasty. The most commanding relic of this section is a huge cross-legged Buddha, 13 metres high, reposing in grotto number 13 and representing a sculptural style which is unique in Yungang. Between its right arm and thigh stands a much smaller statue of a "four-armed strongman". ◁

Grotto Number 5

Linked to grotto number 6, which is the largest in Yungang, this grotto has a four-tiered wooden structure decorating its entrance.

Forming the centrepiece inside is a 17 metre-high sitting Buddha, an image that was probably first sculpted in the art style of the northwest region of China during the Tang dynasty, then remodelled according to the Han school with loose-fitting robes and a long flowing sash. This is one of the more opulent of the Yungang Caves, its walls packed with altars and bas-relief images that reach up to cover the interior of the domed ceiling. The arch doorway is flanked on each side by a Buddha sitting under the bodhi tree. The bas-relief images on the ceiling are renowned for the beauty of their artistic design. △

Wutai Mountain

Thirty-nine monasteries lie within the bounds of Wutai, one of the five mountain ranges which are regarded as Buddhist or Taoist holy places in China. Wutai's five hills are situated in the northeast corner of Wutai County, Shanxi, and their slopes, running with clear streams and covered with lush meadows, stand out in contrast with the generally arid terrain around them. Wutai Mountain was declared a holy place during the East Han dynasty in the years AD 58-75 when an Indian monk visited the region, claimed the mountain as a fitting place in which to worship the Manjusri Bodhisattva, and petitioned the emperor to build a monastery there. ▷

Jinge Temple

Another of the noted Buddhist institutions on Mount Wutai is the Jinge Temple. Built in AD 770 by order of the Tang emperor Daizong, it houses a small bronze figure of the royal patron, while a major part of the temple is devoted to the worship of Guanyin, known as Avalokitesvara Bodhisattva in Sanskrit terminology. Represented as a man until the 12th century, Guanyin became Goddess of Mercy to Buddhists and Taoists in China, protector of children, and saviour of those who suffered misfortune. Here the statue of Guanyin is cast in bronze and clothed in a layer of clay, and is 17 metres tall. A host of attendants flank it on either side. Other deities are worshipped in the other halls, including the 18 arhats and the Buddha of the past, the present and the future, whose statue is located in the main hall at the rear. ▽

Buddha Light Temple

The Fuguang (Buddha Light) Temple, northeast of Wutai County, was one of the major casualties of the brief but violent Tang dynasty crackdown on the Buddhist faith in China. In the year 845, during the reign of Emperor Wuzong, Buddhism was outlawed and the temple destroyed. However, it was rebuilt 12 years later when the religion came back into imperial favour. By then Fuguang, first built between AD 471 and 499 during the rule of the Northern Wei, had a reputation and popularity which extended right across the north of China and even to another main East Asian hotbed of the Buddhist faith, Japan. Today, the temple includes a shrine hall and temple, two pagodas, an excellent array of Tang dynasty clay sculptures and statues of Sakyamuni, Maitreya and Amitabha Buddhas and Vairocana and Manjusri Bodhisattvas. ◁

Sakya Pagoda

This magnificent five-storey pagoda in the Fugong Monastery in Ying County, Shanxi, is the oldest and largest wooden pagoda in China and one of very few ancient wooden structures to have survived earthquakes, fire and other ravages of time. It has been standing for more than 900 years and has been struck by scores of earthquakes, and is still apparently none the worse for wear. Eight-sided with six eaves, its interior construction is quite ingenious — it actually has not five but nine floors inside. Among its most treasured relics is a collection of coloured Buddha images printed with woodblocks on silk, dating back to the Liao dynasty. A gilded statue of Sakyamuni Buddha, 11 metres tall, towers over the altar on the ground floor. ◁

Chongshan Monastery

This monastery in the southeastern district of Taiyuan in Shanxi is thought to have been built during the transition from the Tang to Song dynasties. In 1381 its principal Dabei Hall was added by the third son of the founding emperor of the Ming dynasty, dedicated to the memory of his mother. Inside the prayer hall stands a gilded thousand-hand, thousand-eye Bodhisattva Avalokitesvara with 11 faces, and other Bodhisattva images, all of them standing eight and a half metres tall. A large collection of Song, Yuan and Ming editions of the sutras is kept here, along with a most valuable volume that was printed in 1231 in the reign of the Southern Song ruler, Lizong. ▷

Flying Rainbow Pagoda

The ornate green and polychrome tilework and general design of this pagoda leave visitors in little doubt that its name has something to do with colour. And colour is the dominant theme of the Flying Rainbow Pagoda of the Guangsheng Monastery northeast of Xi'an. The eaves of its first three storeys are packed with exquisitely carved and painted Buddha niches, Bodhisattvas, animals and flowers. Elsewhere, the walls of the rear hall of the monastery's lower section are filled with strikingly coloured murals that look down on Yuan dynasty sculptures of the Amitabha, Maitreya and Sakyamuni Buddhas and various Bodhisattvas and deities. Flying Rainbow Pagoda was first constructed in the Han dynasty and, like many Chinese Buddhist landmarks, rebuilt by the industrious Ming. ▷

Xuanzhong Monastery

This 1,500-year-old-monastery west of Xijiao City in Shanxi had its heyday in the Mongol Yuan dynasty when nearly 40 other monasteries in the region came under its control. It was also regarded as the "ancestral institution" of several eminent monks who promoted the Pure Land sect of Buddhism there — a school of Mahayana in which Nirvana was interpreted as a magnificent paradise or "Pure Land" in the west — and later introduced it to Japan. Some of the remaining shrines and halls of Xuanzhong Monastery belong to the Song era, others to Yuan and Ming, but the Ten-Thousand Buddha Hall and Thousand Buddha Chamber are more recent additions of the Qing dynasty. △ ▷

Xuankong Monastery

The dramatic Xuankong Monastery, which clings to the face of a sheer cliff south of Hunyuan County in Shanxi, is — not surprisingly — called the Hanging in Air Monastery. It is said to have been built in the early 6th century and renovated several times since, each new rebuilding project remaining faithful to the original daring design in which some of the halls and pavilions are only supported by timber piles driven into the rock. A network of narrow paths cut into the cliff face connects the monastery's two principal halls and some 40 other buildings. This astonishing group of buildings has stood firm against centuries of erosion and earthquakes, and its spectacular setting has inspired many poets to write its praise.   ▽

Longmen Caves

The third of the three greatest Buddhist grottoes in China, these caves were dug around the year AD 493 on the bank of the Yi River, south of Luoyang City in Henan. Since then, the cliff has been literally honeycombed with grottoes — well over 2,000 of them containing 100,000 sculptured images, 40 stone towers and 3,600 stone carvings and inscribed steles and plaques. These steles include 30 that feature a variety of styles of calligraphy known as the "Twenty Types at Longmen". Most of the caves date back to the Northern Wei (AD 386-534) and Tang (618-907) eras and feature sculptures of emperors, princes and nobles of those times, alongside the Buddhas.

At the southern end of Longmen, there is a temple named Fengxian. Its construction began in AD 672 during the reign of the Tang emperor, Gaozong, and it took four years to complete this, the largest of the open-air grottoes at Longmen. A donation from the Empress Wu helped the project along. The huge cavern, 35 metres long and 30 metres wide, features nine large Buddha statues, the tallest one standing nearly 18 metres high. It has pronounced Han Chinese Buddha features, with long drooping ears and expressive eyes, and its robes are voluminous. In the north wall of the cave there are statues of a Heavenly Guard and a strongman, both well preserved. The guard supports a pagoda in the palm of its hand, and one of its feet rests heavily on a demon.   ◁ △

White Horse Monastery (Baimasi)

This is the oldest Buddhist institution in China, built in AD 68 just east of what is now the city of Luoyang. And it is linked with the very birth of the Buddhist faith in China. It is said that in AD 64 the Han emperor Ming had a dream in which a golden Buddha flew around his palace. He saw this as a heavenly message, and responded by sending two emissaries to India to seek Buddhist enlightenment. Two Indian monks were also invited to visit China, and they turned up via the Silk Route with Buddhist sutras "carried by white horses". White Horse Monastery was built to celebrate the event.

The monastery has been renovated and expanded over the centuries and its present architecture is the result of extensive work carried out in 1713 in the reign of Emperor Kangxi. The complex is also smaller than the original — which accommodated more than 1,000 monks — and has, of course, lost its early Indian influences. However, there are still some faint traces of Indian design in its Qingliang Terrace, Ganlu Well and Sutra-Burning Terrace. To the east of the monastery stands the Qiyun Pagoda, built in 1175 — a 12-tiered brick tower, 24 metres high, which has weathered the centuries surprisingly well. The graves of the two Indian monks in whose honour the monastery was built lie near the main gate.

Shaolin Monastery

This monastery, built in the time of the Northern Wei dynasty northwest of Dengfeng County in Henan, is considered to be the birthplace of Zen Buddhism. It was constructed in tribute to Bodhidharma, the founder of Zen, who was reputed to be the supreme champion of the martial arts — he taught his disciples the principles of boxing and unarmed combat — and was said to be so light of weight that he crossed the Yangtze River on a flimsy reed. The monastery's heyday was in the Sui and Tang dynasties when it included no less than 5,000 shrines, halls, pagodas and pavilions. Almost all of these have since been demolished, and all that remain of the principal buildings are the Bodhidharma Pavilion, Thousand Buddha Hall, White Robe Hall and Bodhisattva Kitigarbha Hall.

The White Robe Hall, built in the late Qing dynasty, features wall murals depicting various movements and major events of the martial arts, including the epic "Thirteen Monks Rescuing the King of Tang" (pictured below). It is said that the monks, already skilled exponents of kung-fu, joined forces to serve with distinction as retainers of the first Tang emperor. One of the favours they received for their loyalty and protection was permission to build a fortified camp at the monastery.

Some of these monks are buried in the Forest of Stupas (left), featuring some 220 stupas of different architectural styles, that lies to the west of the monastery. In the Thousand Buddha Hall, more evidence of their ancient discipline can be seen — rounded hollows worn in the tiled floor by the constant training that went on over the centuries.

Guanlin

Towering out of farmlands seven kilometres from Luoyang, Guanlin is said to have been the burial place of General Guan Yu of the Three Kingdoms period which followed the Han dynasty. Noted as a brave and efficient soldier, Guan Yu was one of three generals who together established the western kingdom of Shu Han, in what is now modern Sichuan, during the collapse of Han rule. Eventually, one of the three competing kingdoms, the Wei in the north of China, overcame and annexed Shu Han to establish the Wei dynasty. This order was followed by the Jin dynasty, which ruled China for a short period, and some 20 other dynastic orders in which the Han Chinese lost power to various non-Chinese tribal groups such as the Xiongnu, Qiang, Xianbi Badi and Jie. It was not until AD 589, some 250 years after the fall of the Han dynasty, that the reins of power were wrested back into Chinese hands in the Sui dynasty of Emperor Yang Jian.

▽

Fan Pagoda

This hexagonal brick pagoda was built in Kaifeng in the year 977 (Song dynasty) to celebrate the arrival of the Fan family to take up residence in the city. Though otherwise undistinguished, each of its bricks contains a round niche with a carved Buddha in it. At that time, Kaifeng was a great Song dynasty metropolis called Bianjing, and it enjoyed wealth, refinement and expansion until northern tribal pressure on the Song rule led to the dynasty's collapse and the rise of the Jin dynasty based in Hangzhou. Kaifeng has suffered much over the centuries from the calamitous flooding of the nearby Yellow River. Many of its most historic sites were badly damaged or destroyed in the worst floods of 1642, when defenders of the Ming dynasty deliberately breached the dykes protecting the city. ▽

Guanxingtai

This 'Star-Watching Terrace' is the oldest of 27 observatories built throughout China during the reign of the Mongol Yuans. At that time Chinese astronomy had been adapted from the Arabic system and was used in conjunction with the theories and calculations of traditional Chinese astronomers and geomancers to maintain a calendar fortelling the positions of the heavenly bodies and the timing of the seasons — an essential function in the agricultural society and a crucial responsibility of the emperor himself through the astronomical bureau of his Board of Rites in Beijing. In 1610 the system got it wrong, miscalculating an eclipse by several hours, and it gave the Portuguese Jesuits in the imperial court an opportunity to revise the Chinese calendar with modern European methods and to curry added imperial favour for Christianity in China. △

Iron Pagoda (Tieta)

Built in 1049 during the Song dynasty, the Iron Pagoda is so called because of the metallic colour of its tiles. It is a replica of· an earlier wooden structure which was destroyed by fire, and the columns, brackets and rafters decorated with 28 different kinds of tiles faithfully reproduce the details of the original wooden structure. This is an early example of prefabricated construction in the history of Chinese architecture.

Standing more than 50 metres and 13 storeys tall, the pagoda's surface is covered with carved motifs that include flying apsaras, descending dragons, unicorns, lions and Bodhisattvas. Built on rocks on the top of Yi Mountain, the pagoda has firm foundations. The special stairway on the upper part of the pagoda binds the outer walls tightly to the core pillar, thus strengthening the entire structure. ◁▽

Dragon Pavilion (Longting)

Looking almost like a pavilion of Beijing's Forbidden City, Dragon Pavilion lies between two ornamental lakes in Kaifeng. It was built in the final Qing dynasty on what is thought to have been the site of the palace of the Northern Song emperor. The pavilion stands on a raised brick dais with a double roof, yellow-glazed tiles and red pillars and walls. Among its relics is a cube decorated with carved dragons which is thought to have been the Song emperor's throne. Its two nearby lakes are called Yang and Pan, and have become part of local folklore. Yang is a clear lake, and is named after a family who are said to have lived beside it and were noted for their loyalty to the emperor. The Pan lake is muddy, reflecting, it is said, the treachery of the disloyal Pans who also lived on its shore.
△ ▷

Qiaolou Hall

Originally built at the end of the 6th century, Qiaolou Hall, the main building of the Fuqing Monastery, was reconstructed at the start of the Qing dynasty. The decorative ceramic figurines and animals placed on the green and yellow tiled roof and the painting in Su style on the columns and beams are typical of the architectural design in the early Qing period.

The hall perches on a single-arched stone bridge high over a deep ravine. The bridge is 15 metres long and 9 metres wide. Looking down the gorge from the hall, the trees and grass below appear to be a sea of green. The sky above seems so close that one can almost touch the floating clouds.

The gateway to the monastery, at the top of a long flight of steps on the north side of Cangyan Mountain, bears a welcoming couplet: "The hall has no lamps, the moon illuminates it; the gateway is unlocked, the clouds seal it."

▽

Cangyan Mountain

Cangyan Mountain in Jinging County, Hebei is an extension of the Taihang Mountain Range.

It is noted for its harmonious blending of nature and art. Exquisitely designed monasteries and studios are interspersed among the foliage of

pines and white sandalwood, rugged rocks and cascading streams.

In a precarious but well-protected setting, Fuqing Monastery clings to the upper ledge of one of the mountain's sheer cliff faces.

The curved tile roof of the temple is typical of traditional Chinese architecture. The curved roof evolved in the Song dynasty, an age in which art and architecture flourished, and became more and more flamboyant over the ensuing centuries. Ornate and sometimes garish ornaments were placed at either end of the roof ridge, and animal sculptures on the eaves to ward off evil spirits. Roofs were originally thatched, but were gradually tiled with glazed terra cotta or porcelain in the distinctive semi-cylindrical design that is said to have been based on split bamboo. △

Zhaozhou Bridge

Also known as Anji Bridge, this is unquestionably one of the world's great masterpieces of bridge-building technology — and it was constructed nearly 1,400 years ago. The Zhaozhou Bridge, built between AD 605 and 618, is single-spanned and more than 50 metres long. It is celebrated not only for its long span, and for the incomparable beauty and economy of its design, but also for the innovative engineering of its segmental arches.

Two pairs of segmental arches stand on the main arch in the spandrels to reduce the load of the spandrel masonry and provide an overflow for floodwaters. It was not until the 14th century that this "open spandrel" technique was adopted in European bridge-building, 700 years after the construction of Zhaozhou. Despite constant use for many centuries the bridge has weathered well without major renovation. Some of the original posts and beautifully carved panels of the balustrades were lost over the centuries,

crumbling away and falling into the river, and in 1953 some of these were dug out of the mud of the riverbed and reinstalled.

△

Lugou Bridge

Marco Polo called this "the finest bridge in the world", which it undoubtedly was when it was completed in the year 1193. In those days the Chinese were nearly 1,000 years ahead of the Europeans, and indeed the rest of the world, in many fields of engineering and science. The bridge was repaired in the Ming dynasty, and then, after having been badly damaged by floods, was re-built in 1698 (the 37th year of the Qing emperor Kangxi). Now it remains a fine and remarkably strong structure as well as a unique architectural relic.

Spanning the Yongding River southwest of Beijing, Lugou Bridge is 266 metres long with 11 arches. It was designed so that it could withstand the force of wind and ice. However, even more famous than its design are the stone carvings on the bridge. There are 485 vividly carved stone lions, all in different postures, forming a kind of ceremonial guard along the balustrades — in fact, there are so many of them that the phrase "stone lions of Lugou Bridge" has come to mean anything of which there are "so many that one loses count". ▽▷

The Ancient Palaces

Better known all over the world as Beijing's Forbidden City, the Ancient Palaces were the residence and political nerve-centre of the emperors of the Ming and succeeding Manchu Qing dynasties, and the hotbed of intrigue among their huge courts. The original palaces, which took 15 years to build, were started in 1406 by the third emperor of the Ming dynasty, Chengzu, when he moved the imperial capital to Beijing. The complex, the largest surviving cluster of wooden buildings on such a scale in the world, has since played a central role in the most momentous phases of contemporary Chinese history — the wealth, power and glory of the Ming, the Manchu triumph of the Qing dynasty, then its gradual decay in the face of foreign pressure and incursion, and finally the complete collapse of the dynastic order. After the fall of the Manchus and establishment of the short-lived Chinese republic, the Forbidden City fell into disrepair but was restored in the 1950s according to its original plans — the spirits of 24 great and not-so-great divine rulers of China's immense past still facing south, according to ancient Chinese geomancy, and their people facing north in obeisance.

148

Wumen

This gigantic terrace, on which stands the "Five Phoenix" Mansions, is the main front entrance to the Forbidden City. Wumen (Midday Gate) is where the emperors issued edicts, had miscreant mandarins publicly flogged and presided over the execution of common criminals sharp at noon. Built in 1420 and rebuilt in 1647, it is actually five gateways, the central one reserved for the emperor's carriages. Once inside, visitors and emissaries proceeded to the Taihe Hall, where the rulers conducted state ceremonies and political business, or to the Baohe Hall which was the setting for state banquets and, at one time, the examination hall for civil service candidates. Another mansion, Zhonghe Hall, was where the emperors studied briefing papers before attending meetings in the Taihe Hall. An inner section of the palaces, north of Baohe Hall, included the emperor's living quarters and Imperial Garden.

◁ ▽

Qianqing Hall

This Qing dynasty reception and banqueting hall also served a crucial role in the security and harmony of the dynastic order. It was where the Qing emperors chose their successors. From the time of Emperor Yongzheng, who assumed the throne in 1723, it was the custom for each ruler to write the name of his intended successor on two pieces of paper, one to be kept in his personal possession and the other secreted behind a plaque bearing the inscription "upright and bright". Upon the emperor's death his closest ministers would compare the two names, and if they tallied they announced the new ruler. More than 40 mansions surround the Qianqing Hall, some of them containing the emperor's crown and robes of office and books and artworks, others in which he held audiences with his chief scholars and advisers; and still others which were reading rooms, medical consulting rooms and living quarters for the imperial servants, maids, concubines and palace eunuchs.

▽

Corner Pavilion

The Forbidden City was so called because the common people were forbidden to enter it, and observation and security towers placed at each corner of the 150,000 square metre palace grounds made certain that all but the aristocracy were kept out. These pavilions were based on the designs of the "Yellow Crane" and "Prince Teng" Mansions of the Song dynasty, and today their complex and extravagant roof structures are regarded as yet another masterpiece of traditional architecture. △

The Summer Palace

The powerful and ruthless Empress Dowager (Cixi), the last real dynastic ruler of China, built the Summer Palace in 1888 on the site of a previous palace and garden that had dated from the Jin dynasty. The project has since been regarded as something of an extravagant folly. For one thing, the empress appropriated much of the cost of it, some 24 million taels of silver, from funds set up to modernise the Chinese navy — and was soon to see the navy, or fleets of magnificent but obsolete and outgunned war-junks, suffer a humiliating defeat under the guns and rockets of a British iron-hulled steam-paddle warship brought from England to smash open the doors to free trade in China. As for the Summer Palace itself, Allied Forces gutted and plundered it two years after it had been completed, and a subsequent rebuilding project only added to its vast cost. Nowadays its lake, gardens, shrines and pavilions are open to the public, along with another symbol of the Empress Dowager's stubborn extravagance, the giant Marble Boat on Kunming Lake, a stone replica of a showboat paddle steamer.

A bronze pavilion, called Pavilion of Precious Clouds is another feature of the Summer Palace. It was cast in 1750 and reaches a height of nearly eight metres and weighs over 200 tons. ◁

Kunming Lake

A number of streams from the western districts of Beijing, including one called Jade Spring Mountain, were channelled by engineers of the Yuan dynasty to form the great lake of the Summer Palace. The Qing emperor, Qianlong, gave it its name when he refurbished a Ming dynasty palace and temple, the Duabao Pagoda, to celebrate his mother's 60th birthday. Later, the Empress Dowager added much of the rest of the construction around the lake, including the Palace Which Dispels Clouds, which she built to celebrate her own birthday. ▽

The Long Gallery

This corridor, 728 metres long, follows the line of the northern bank of Kunming Lake and is designed to reflect its special blend of architecture and nature in the still waters around it. Its ceiling is also painted with some 8,000 "still life" compositions of flowers and scenes from famous Chinese stories and legends, and for this reason it is also called the Picture Corridor. Halfway along the gallery lies the Empress Dowager's opulent Palace Which Dispels Clouds; further along stands the beautiful Listening to Orioles Hall (Tingliguan), now a seafood restaurant; and at the end of the corridor the garish white Marble Boat reflects the sudden twist of refinement to vulgarity that took place in the Empress Dowager's reign. △

Temple of Heaven

Tiantan, the Temple of Heaven, in the southwestern corner of Beijing, is an ensemble of shrines, and was once the venue for the most important imperial rites — prayers for good harvest, sacrifices to the gods and royal ancestors and communion with the heavens. Built in 1420 (the 18th year of the reign of the Ming emperor Yongle), the building is part of a series of four temples in Beijing representing the firmament, the others being the Temple of the Sun, the Temple of the Earth and the Temple of the Moon. The buildings are spaced out over an area of more than 2,700,000 square metres, and altogether took 14 years to build.

The Temple of Heaven consists of two main structures linked by a 360-metre long bridge. It is regarded as a most remarkable architectural composition in which mathematical balance and economy of design have achieved an almost overwhelming majesty. It is also a masterpiece of acoustics, its most novel feature being a circular wall of polished bricks in Huangqiong House (Imperial Vault of Heaven), where echoes run clearly

Qiniandian

This, the Temple for Praying for a Good Harvest, shown at left and with a detail of its domed ceiling, dominates the Temple of Heaven from the top of three concentric terraces fenced with carved white marble balustrades. It is where the emperor came each year at the first full moon for fertility rites that go back to the distant beginnings of Chinese history. At the winter solstice he would also mount the three terraces of the Circular Sacrificial Altar where, after much prayer and traditional clay pipe music, a young bullock would be sacrificed to the gods. As such, the emperor was the vital conduit between the teeming Chinese society and the spiritual forces that ruled much of its existence. Though sometimes a harsh and despotic ruler himself, he was also servant of two masters — acting as the vehicle through which the people's fears and wishes were made known to the heavenly deities, and a kind of human lightning rod for bolts of good fortune or retribution from on high. ◁

from one end to another, giving it the name Echo Wall. This hall also contains sacred ancestral tablets, as well as those dedicated to the gods of rain, the sun, the moon, the stars, dawn, the wind, thunder and lightning. When Western troops invaded Beijing in 1860 and 1900, the Temple of Heaven suffered serious damage, and it was not until 1918 that the temple was repaired and reopened to the public. ▷

Shifangpujue Monastery

Located on the southern slope of Shouan Hill just outside Beijing, this monastery was first built in the Tang dynasty in the 7th century, and rebuilt in 1734 (the 12th year of the Qing emperor Yongzheng). It is also called the Sleeping Buddha Monastery because it houses a reclining statue of Buddha. The main feature of this symmetrically designed monastery is the Hall of the Sleeping Buddha, where a bronze image of Sakyamuni lies in an apparent state of Nirvana. The statue, cast in 1321 in the Yuan dynasty, is more than five metres long, and depicts Sakyamuni speaking with his disciples about his impending departure from all earthly things. Lying on one side, with his right hand pitched against his head, the Buddha is the very picture of ease and calm, attended by disciples represented here as 12 clay statues standing behind him. △

Maitreya Buddha

Standing 26 metres high and carved from a single trunk of sandalwood, this statue of the Maitreya is housed in the Yonghe Palace in Beijing. Originally built by the Qing emperor Yongzheng as a palace, Yonghe was presented to lama priests in 1740 and is also known as the Lama Temple. ▽

Yonghe Palace

The Qing emperor Yongzheng lived in this complex first as a prince and later as emperor, using parts of the premises for the practice of Tibetan Buddhism. When the emperor died, his coffin was lodged here, and the green roof-tiles were replaced by yellow ones, whereby the place was officially elevated to the rank of a palace for housing Yongzheng's image and for the ancestral worship of the royal Qing house. The palace was presented to the lamas by Emperor Qianlong in 1744 and turned into a lamasery, and it stands today as the largest and one of the best-preserved Buddhist institutions in China. In the five halls that make up the monastery, valuable Buddhist images in bronze and stone stand alongside rare relics of the Yellow Sect of Tibetan Buddhism, including ancient copies of the Tripitaka sutras. Its walls contain many colourful murals of Buddhist stories and Buddha images, such as the white portrait of the Avalokitesvara Bodhisattva in the picture above. The many siderooms also house valuable collections of Buddhist scriptures and writings in mathematics, medicine, astronomy and geography.

◁ △

Biyun Monastery

When Buddhism first took root in China its architecture naturally followed the style of that of its birthplace, India. But almost all early Chinese construction was of wood, and the evidence of whole periods of history was destroyed by fire. Through a combination of reconstruction and its own artistic development, Han Chinese architecture soon dominated the design of religious and public buildings. A group of white marble pagodas remains, however, as a striking example of early Indian design in the Biyun Monastery on the eastern slope of Fragrant Hill in Beijing. The tallest is 13-tiered and 35 metres high and is decorated with Tibetan Buddhist themes in bas-relief. ▷

Glazed Pagoda of Xiangshan

This beautiful green pagoda is eight-sided and seven-tiered but only 10 metres tall. It stands in Xiangshan Park in Beijing and was built in typical Qing dynasty fashion, with a combination of stone tiles and wooden corridors and 56 bronze wind-bells tinkling from its many eaves. It is the only structure to survive inside the Zhao Temple, which was built in 1780 (the 45th year of the reign of the Qing emperor Qianlong) in the Tibetan style of architecture, and served as a guesthouse to the sixth Panchen Lama when he visited Beijing. The pagoda, which lies to the west of it, is now regarded as the emblem of this complex.

▽

Little Garden of Qianlong

Nature and the architect's vision have blended splendidly to create this garden within a garden, originally called Jingxinzhai, or "Quiet Mind Studio", on the northern shore of Beihai in Beijing. It features elaborate formations of rocks from Lake Tai in artificial hills and craggy shorelines around the garden's lotus and lily covered ponds, and a series of peaceful pavilions and water bowers. Constructed in 1758, the Little Garden was completely renovated in 1913 after the fall of the dynastic order and the setting up of the Chinese republic, and was used as a reception venue for foreign diplomats.

◁

Northsea (Beihai) Park

For more than 1,000 years the North Sea Park — as mundane as its name may be — was the royal garden of successive dynasties that included the Liao, Jin, Yuan and Ming. It covers an area of 700,000 square metres, and among its beautifully landscaped gardens, hillocks and pools there are two particular artistic attractions. One, the famous Nine Dragon Wall, is a 26 metre-long ceramic monument made up of 424 seven-coloured glazed tiles depicting nine dragons in high relief on each side. The other showpiece is the White Stupa (or Dagoba) which is a prime example of Tibetan Buddhist architecture. Built in 1651, it was badly damaged by earthquakes in 1679 and 1731.　　△▷

Buddha Tooth Sarira Pagoda

According to the Buddhist chronicles, when Sakyamuni Buddha died two particles of Sarira (Sheli) from his teeth were found in the cremation ashes. One of them was taken to the "Lion Country" or what is now Sri Lanka, and the other was saved by the monk Faxian. It was installed as a highly sacred relic in a temple that stood where the Sarira Pagoda has since been built.

Sarira, a word derived from Sanskrit, is the technical term for what is recognised as the highest and most developed state of spiritual life — the state in which the vital physical juices are transformed into small brilliant "jewels" that are found in the ashes after the cremation fires have done their work. The name is used also simply to designate a relic, and pagodas and shrines in which Sheli jewels are kept are held in high esteem. △ ▷

Ming Tombs (Shisanling)

Ranking with the Forbidden City and the Great Wall as one of the most renowned monuments to Chinese imperial history, the Ming Tombs lie in the shadow of Tianshou Mountain 50 kilometres north of Beijing. They were built as mausoleums for 13 emperors of the Ming dynasty from the reign of Chengzue to Sizong, covering a period of more than 200 years from 1409 to 1644. The approach to the tombs alone is monumental — an 11-storey white marble memorial archway with five gates and six pillars is the main entrance; beyond it stands the Dahong Gate (Red Main Gate) with red walls and yellow roof tiles; and beyond that lies a wide seven-kilometre Road of the Gods lined with large stone sculptures of lions, camels, elephants, unicorns and horses and statues of court officials in the ceremonial dress, each slightly bowed in a gesture of respect. The tombs of the emperors and their consorts are found in the Baocheng (Precious) City, each surrounded by a red wall and each containing a particular stone tablet which, unlike the others, has nothing inscribed upon it — symbolising the infinite beneficence of the imperial rulers. ◁

Chang Tomb (Changling)

No other tomb ranks in size and grandeur with the Chang Tomb, built in 1413 for the Emperor Yongle. Its Lingen Hall stands on a three metre-high white marble podium, covers an area of 1,900 square metres and is supported by 32 timber columns which, five centuries later, are every bit as sturdy and well preserved as when they were installed. Chang Tomb is the first mausoleum to have been built, and it set the standard of design for the 12 other tombs that followed. ▽

Ding Tomb (Dingling)

Lying southwest of Chang Tomb below the Dayu Hill, Ding Tomb was built for Emperor Shenzong and his two queens — started in 1584 when he was still alive, it was completed six years later. It features the Brilliant Tower, roofed with yellow-glazed cylindrical tiles and stone tablets inscribed with the words "Da Ming" (Great Ming) and "Tomb of Shenzong", but otherwise there is little surface evidence of the far grander spectacle that lies under the ground behind this mausoleum entrance. △

The Underground Palace

Behind the Brilliant Tower of Ding Tomb lies the Underground Palace, or burial tomb, of Emperor Shenzong and his two queens, the only burial hall excavated so far in the Ming Tombs. Archeologists broke through to it in 1956 and found five chambers, each separated by a four-tonne stone door, that were as majestic as any of the Pharaonic tombs unearthed in Egypt. Under the vast domed ceiling of the stone hall they found the coffins of Shenzong and his wives, along with golden crowns and other ceremonial headwear, porcelain, utensils, jade

vases, silkwear and other burial possessions — the stone funerary bed lying in surroundings of bare simplicity compared with the decor and furnishings of the adjoining chambers. There, the floors are paved with "gold" tiles impregnated with tung oil to give them a lasting lustre, and the central chamber features intricately carved white marble benches, blue porcelain urns with dragon motifs and other Ming dynasty artwork. ▷

Qingdong Mausoleums

The Qing dynasty buried its emperors on a series of sites, the earliest of them in the Qingdong Tombs in Zunhua County, 125 kilometres east of Beijing — a cluster of mausoleums that developed into the most extensive burial spot in China. The tombs were commenced in 1663 and Emperors Shunzhi, Kangxi, Qianlong, Xianfeng, and Tongzhi along with their consorts and more than 100 concubines were laid to rest. Though not as ornate as the preceding Ming dynasty tombs, these burial places followed basically the same pattern of Great Red Gate entrances opening on to sacred avenues — a six-kilometre approach in this case — lined with stone sculptures of animals and statues of civil and military officers. ◁

Yu Mausoleum

The largest of the Qingdong tombs is that of Emperor Shunzhi, but the most impressive are those of Qianlong (below) and the Empress Dowager Cixi. The interior walls of both tombs are richly carved and gilded, and the empress's resting place features many Buddha images, reflecting the devoutly religious side of her otherwise stubborn and imperious character. ▽

Dule Monastery

The Tang emperor Xuanzong and his beloved concubine Yang not only enjoyed a torrid love affair that was immortalised in the poem "Song of Everlasting Sorrow" — the emperor devoted so much of his time and energy to the affair that it led to a rebellion led by one of his brothers-in-law, An Lushan. The revolt ended tragically for the emperor — he was forced to witness the execution of the woman whose charms had drawn him away from the vital affairs of state. Dule Monastery stands where An Lushan is said to have launched his insurrection, and is also known as Enjoy Alone Monastery because of the rebel leader's habit of keeping himself to himself. The monastery features a 23 metre-high Guanyin Hall, built without a single nail, and a 16 metre clay Guanyin statue with 10 Buddha heads which is the tallest clay sculpture in China. ▽▷

Qingxi Mausoleums

Other Qing dynasty monarchs, the Emperors Yongzheng, Jiaqing, Daoguang and Guangxu, were buried in the Qingxi tombs, a resting place covering half a million square metres in Yi County, Hebei. The tombs here are more scattered than those at Qindong Tombs but are considered architecturally more interesting and are set against a pleasant backdrop of wooded hills. Emperor Guangxu's death and burial was shrouded in intrigue and scandal. Although he was the second last emperor of China, the imperial power really lay in the hands of the Empress Dowager, who stamped on any 20th century reforms that he attempted to promote, imprisoned him in the Summer Palace and finally ordered his assassination in 1908 just before she herself died. △

169

Baotu Spring

Jinan City in Shandong Province is famous, among other things, for no less than 72 springs which gush up from a huge subterranean reservoir. The most celebrated of them is Baotu Spring which has three "eyes" from which the water erupts in three fountains — a phenomenon which the famous calligrapher and painter, Zhao Mengfu of the Yuan dynasty, pictured as a white jade vase gushing out of the flat ground. The water is considered ideal for the making of tea, which by the Tang dynasty had become China's national beverage and such a ceremony and art that, simply to take a drink of it, the socially refined were advised to follow seven steps in the brewing and use 24 implements in the preparation and serving — and to forget it altogether if even one of these was missing.   △

Daming Lake

Lying north of Jinan, Daming Lake is a small body of water with a big history — a former pleasure spot for the educated classes of old Chinese society, and mentioned in a book written as far back as the 4th century. Its Lixia Pavilion which stands on an island in the middle was a favourite meeting place of the Tang dynasty poet Du Fu and Li Yong, the prefect of Beihai, and paintings of them are on display there. Around the lake there are other historic buildings, a Yuan dynasty pavilion and a memorial temple to the Song dynasty governor of Jinan, the scholar Zeng Gong. ◁ △

Thousand Buddha Hill

Remarkable Buddha images, carved into the rock, are a feature of Thousand Buddha Hill, just south of Jinan. The spot is also called Emperor Shun Farming Hill because it was said that the legendary ruler, believed to have lived 4,000 to 5,000 years ago, grew the grain here with which he introduced his people to the principle of barter. A monastery, Xingguo, stands on the peak of the hill, with a gate inscribed with a couplet that reads:

"The evening drums and morning bells shake up the people who hanker after profit and fame.
The sutra-chanting and Buddha-prayers call back the people from the sea of bitterness and confusion."

The monastery's East Temple (Lis-

hanyuan) was designed to embrace all the three principal faiths, Buddhism, Taoism and Confucianism.

Tai Mountain

Tai Mountain is another of the five most sacred mountains in China, associated with the father of Chinese social philosophy, Confucius, who was born in Shandong Province. For centuries — more than 40 of them — Chinese from the lowliest coolie to the emperors themselves have made pilgrimages to its 1,545 metre main peak. At the foot of the mountain there is Taishan Temple, which was built in the Han reign and added to in the Tang and Song dynasties. Climbing the hill is no easy feat — a total of 7,200 steps have to be negotiated to reach the South Sky Gate which opens on to the summit.

From there, and its beautiful Jade Emperor Hall, visitors can enjoy four "famous sights" — "The Sun Rising on Tai Mountain", "Evening Colours", "Golden Ribbon of the Yellow River" and "Sea of Clouds".

Triumphal Gateway to Tai Mountain

A three-arched triumphal gateway (pailou) at the foot of Tai Mountain marks the spot where Confucius is said to have rested before making his own pilgrimage to the summit nearly 2,500 years ago. On the peak, an outcrop of rock features inscriptions by other illustrious visitors, various emperors going back to the infatuated and ill-fated Xuanzong of the Tang dynasty. ◁ △

Black Dragon Pond (Heilongtan)

This body of water on the western approach to Tai Mountain creates a dramatic and picturesque waterfall, and a popular picnic spot, below the arch of a 23 metre single-span bridge. ▷

Forest of Confucius (Konglin)

This, probably the most significant historic site in China, is where Confucius and his descendants were buried. It lies one and a half kilometres north of Qufu City in Shandong; an ornate roofed gateway leading to the Forest of Confucius, a huge grove of 20,000 old and rare trees, some of which it is claimed were planted by Confucian disciples over the centuries. Aside from Confucian shrines and other buildings, the complex includes the Xiang Hall, constructed in the Ming dynasty for sacrificial rites, and the tomb of a celebrated writer, Kong Shangren, who penned the drama *Peach-Blossom Fan*.

△

Confucius Residence

Since Confucius set the ethical guidelines of Chinese society more than two millennia ago, successive dynasties have paid tribute to him and his descendants by bestowing honorary nobility on them and maintaining and expanding the master's residence. The present Confucius Residence, as it is called, was built in the Song dynasty between 1038 and 1039 and has burgeoned in the centuries since then to include 460 buildings, including halls, chambers and living quarters. All for the spirit of an ancient, albeit revered man. Each dynasty has also contributed some of the finest artworks of its period as furnishings and decoration, and Confucius Residence houses a priceless collection of porcelain and other ceramics, costumes, bronzes, weapons, furniture, screens, scrolls and calligraphy.

▷

The Confucius Grave

After the death of Confucius in 479 BC, his disciples kept watch on his grave for three years. And according to the *Shiji (Annals of History)* by Sima Qian, one particular devotee, Zigong, carried on the vigil alone for another three years to demonstrate his love for the master and grief at his passing. To the west of the Confucius Grave in the Forest of Confucius there is a terrace and three cottages bearing a tablet inscribed with the words "This is where Zigong kept watch."

The grave itself has the burial spot of Confucius's son to its east and that of his grandson to the south, conforming to the traditional burial pattern of "carrying a son and grandson". A measure of the abiding devotion to Confucius is a one-kilometre ceremonial avenue leading to the gravesite, flanked with all the imperial trappings of stone animal sculptures and statues of military heroes. △

Confucian Temple

Two years after Confucius died the Prince of Lu ordered the building of a temple on the original site of the great sage's house, declaring it a monument to the philosopher and a place of worship. Later dynastic rulers added their own memorials, shrines and halls to the temple, eventually establishing a complex that covers about 220,000 square metres and is one of the most palatial sacred institutions in China. The Apricot Auditorium (Xingtan) pictured on the opposite page is said to have been built on the spot where Confucius held discussion meetings with his disciples. The temple's principal hall, Dacheng, houses a clay sculpture of Confucius surrounded by images of his 12 closest followers and latter-day sages such as Yan Hui, Zeng Zi and Mencius. Inside another hall, Shengji, there are 120 engraved stone panels illustrating the great man's life.

Lao Mountain

Lao Mountain, a rocky mountain near the Shandong seaside resort and port of Qingdao, is another of China's sacred peaks. On its slopes there is a spring called Divine Spring which, it is said, has never dried up, even in the most severe drought, and was regarded as the elusive and much-coveted Elixir of Life by the ancients. Certainly, the first emperor of Qin, and Emperor Wu of the Han dynasty, are said to have visited Lao Mountain in search of the immortalising potion. The mountain is also revered by Taoists as the home of many Immortals. Among its temples and monasteries the most sacred is Tai-qing Palace, first built in 140 BC during the reign of the Han emperor, Wu. ◁

Dragon and Tiger Pagoda

This pagoda, 11 metres high, stands in Licheng County and is so called because of the dragon and tiger motifs carved into its faces. The dragon, far from being the mythical horror of the medieval West, is associated with strength, goodness and the very spirit of life in China. The *Shuowen Dictionary*, written in AD 200, states that of the 369 species of fish and reptiles in China the dragon is king, representing the spirit of changing nature — "His voice is heard in the hurricane which, scattering the withered leaves of the forest, quickens a new spring." ▷

Penglai Mansions

The Eight Immortals, or Baxian, are legendary beings of the Taoist religion who are said to have achieved immortality through their discovery of the inner secrets of nature. They are also said to have the power of raising the dead, along with a "Midas touch" that will turn anything into gold.

Erected on the hills of Danya in Penglai County of Shantung Province, Penglai Mansions is a series of Taoist temples and monasteries said to be the Land of the Immortals. Perched above the Yellow Sea, usually enshrouded in mist, the mansions appear to be unreal.

This is also the scene of an occasional optical illusion, something like a desert mirage, in which the landscape and landmarks of areas 100 kilometres away will appear over the waters. The mirages are frequent at the end of spring and at the beginning of the summer season, and are particularly spectacular on a clear day following a rainstorm. In ancient times it was believed that these mirages spouted from the mouths of sea monsters.

Old Man Rock

Rising abruptly from the seas off the port of Qingdao, Old Man Rock represents wisdom and stoicism in the winds and tides of life. Age is highly respected in China, and longevity is a passion. The star-god of longevity is Canopus in the constellation of Argo — "gentle and smiling, his venerable head, monstrously high on the brow with white hair and eyebrows, mounted or leaning upon a stag". He is often pictured holding a peach or in the most auspicious company of the star-gods of wealth and happiness. ◁

Water City

This huge fortification, running from the base of the eastern slope of Danya Hill in Shandong's Penglai County, was built in 1376 as a defence against Japanese pirate raids. When first constructed in the reign of the Ming ruler Taizu, it was simply a sea wall of rammed earth. Two centuries later, in the reign of Shenzong, it was completely rebuilt with rock foundations and brick walls. It is 2,200 metres long and stands seven metres high.

An ingeniously designed embankment dividing Water City into two halves provided an ideal place for the training of the navy and the mooring of vessels. The embankment regulated the flow of currents and tides, and maintained the water level within the sheltered area for the smooth manoeuvring of vessels entering and leaving Water City.

It remained an important naval base during the Ming and Qing dynasties because of its strong fortifications and strategic position. ◁

Qingdao Pier

This structure is as much a symbol of Qingdao as the local spring water, which is one of the ingredients of the popular Qingdao beer. Built in 1931, it is 440 metres long and runs out to a semi-circular jetty on which stands an eight-cornered, two-storey pavilion called Huilan. Qingdao was a small fishing village until Song dynasty engineers developed its harbour to handle the trade of the Shandong hinterland. In the 1890s the Germans grabbed it as a trading concession and naval base. Japan wanted it next, demanding it at the beginning of World War One, and it was not until 1922 that it was returned to Chinese sovereignty. Today it is a popular resort, being one of China's few seaside spots with broad sandy beaches suitable for safe bathing and suntanning. ▷

The Yellow River

The Yellow River is China's second largest river, 5,464 kilometres long and winding through the provinces and autonomous zones of Qinghai, Sichuan, Gansu, Ningxia, Inner Mongolia, Shaanxi, Shanxi, Henan and Shandong before flowing into the Bo Sea. It has over 30 main tributaries and countless minor streams covering an area of 750,000 square kilometres. It waters the vast loess tableland of central China, picking up immense amounts of sand and mud that colour its waters yellow and give it the highest volume of alluvial deposits of any river in the world.

This combination of enormous water volume and silt has, since time immemorial, made the Yellow River both benefactor and scourge of the millions of people living along its banks. In its lower reaches, near its estuary, it has often burst its banks or suddenly changed course altogether because of silt deposits, flooding large areas of land and killing many thousands of people. But it has also provided abundant water and fertile soil for agricultural settlement that may well have been the first to appear on earth.

"Peking Man" has shown that human settlement had been established in the Yellow River Basin half a million years ago. At Banbo in Xi'an, excavation has unearthed a Neolithic village dating back some 6,000 years, and

Neolithic pottery, carved tortoise shells (used as writing tablets in ancient times) and carved ox-bones have been found in Henan Province. But an even more exciting find was made in 1963 when the fossilised remains of "Lantian Man" were unearthed in Shaanxi province and proved to be a full 100,000 years older than "Peking Man". Elsewhere in China, remains have been found of a proto-human or forerunner of man who existed 1.7 million years ago, and there is little doubt that these "ape-men" also roamed the fertile and food-rich banks and alluvial plains of the Yellow River.

But that which the Yellow River has given humanity it has also, to a much lesser extent, taken away. Its terrible floods have given it the reputation of being "China's sorrow", wreaking untold disaster almost every year. According to records, over a period of 2,000 years the river has flooded more than 1,500 times, and there have been 26 occasions on which it has completely changed its course. An indication of the violence with which it switched direction comes from records that show its course at one point in history as flowing around to the north of the Shandong Mountains, then into the Bo Sea, and at another point cutting south of them to join the Huai River and emptying into the Yellow Sea — the distance between the two estuaries being about 500 kilometres.

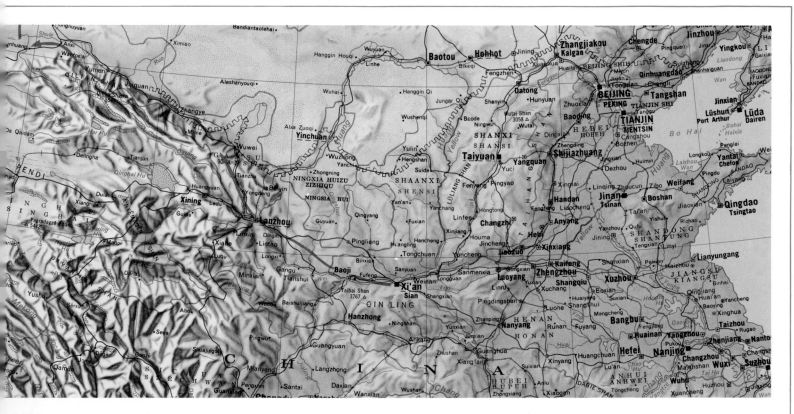

Bayanhar Mountains

This confluence of three mountain ranges is the watershed between the Yellow and the Yangtze Rivers. Bayanhar Mountains, a branch of the Kunlun Range, lie 6,000 metres above sea level and are capped with snow most of the year. The northern slopes are easily accessible, while the southern slopes are full of ravines.

Despite their beauty — their Mongolian name means "the fertile mountains of dark green" — the upper slopes are cold, rocky and desolate with only sparse patches of grassland supporting a thin scattering of Tibetan nomads and their cattle and sheep. But when summer comes, the mountains' many glaciers, and the lower melting snows, send hundreds of streams into the muddy sweep of the Yellow and Yangtze Rivers.   ▽

Jishi Mountains

Close to its source in Qinghai Province, the Yellow River takes shape as it emerges from the Gyaring Lake and becomes a river 50 to 60 metres wide and one metre deep — its waters so crystal clear that it is like glass. Jishi Mountains extend from southeast Qinghai to the southern borders of Gansu Province and include the Maqen Gangri Peak, 6,282 metres high and permanently snow-capped. The Tibetans call Jishi Mountain the "ancestor of the Yellow River". After passing this range the river flows into Gansu and then turns on a wide loop back into Qinghai Province Its waters then enter the loess region, and their pristine clarity turns to a silt-laden yellow murk. ▽

Upper Yellow River

The up-river section of the Yellow River begins at a place called Guide, where the waters crash down through two major gorges to flatten out in Xunhua, one of the 18 counties of Qinghai. For most of this stretch, the river is expansive and slow-moving with a backdrop of craggy mountains. But beyond Xunhua it speeds up again into a rushing torrent, forced through some 19 gorges in Gansu Province and unnavigable for much of its flow. About 80 percent of Qinghai's 1.8 million population live along the course of the Yellow River. ▷

Liujia Gorge

Liujia Gorge is probably the most spectacular spot along the upper course of the Yellow River. It is the point where the river takes a full 90-degree turn to the west on the border between Qinghai and Gansu Provinces. The gorge can be reached by boat, and to many visitors the scene is reminiscent of the beautiful and strangely shaped outcrops of Guilin in the south. At this point on its course, the river is already taking on its "yellow" hue, but the quantity of silt in it is only about five percent, even in flooding. Most of the silt is dumped into it by its tributaries, which in this area are the Tao, Datong and Huang Shui. △

Yellow River Bridge at Lanzhou

This, the first steel bridge on the Yellow River, was built in 1907 by a German company and it cost 306,000 taels of silver. It replaced a pontoon bridge that had served as a crossing since 1398 in the Ming period. According to the *Lanzhou Prefecture Gazette* some 24 large boats were used as pontoons, and the whole structure was dismantled each winter when the waters froze over and horses and carriages could get across. △

Qingtong Gorge

When the Yellow River leaves the gorge region in Gansu and flows into Ningxia Huizu Autonomous Region, it is flanked on one side by the Tengger Desert and on the other by mountainous border areas. Qingtong Gorge lies in the middle of Ningxia, six kilometres long and cutting the Yinchuan Plain into north and south regions. It is a strategic area and was the site of many famous battles to protect the heartland of China, including those fought under General Ma Xian of the Han dynasty and the Tang general Li Jing. They were fierce and dangerous encounters, and two lines from an ancient poem tell why:

"Soldiers sent to fight in Qingtong Gorge, Nine out of ten will never return." ◁

Baotou

It is in Inner Mongolia that the Yellow River begins causing its proverbial sorrow, reaching the area called Baotou and broadening out until it is nearly three kilometres wide and very slow-moving. When it reaches flood level it is like a vast inland sea, and it changes course very often, causing disastrous flooding. North of Baotau, the area of He Tao reflects the river's two faces of wrath and benevolence. The name Tao is referred to in an old proverb: "The Yellow River has a hundred harmful ways, but the Tao is rich" — thus contrasting the flood danger with the flat, fertile land that the river has formed around He Tao and which was farmed as far back as the Qin and Han dynasties. In those days He Tao was known as the "Granary of the Frontiers". ▽

Fenglin Ford

Fenglin Ford is where the Yellow River turns east at an important crossroads between Shanxi, Shaanxi and Henan Provinces. The crossing is provided by a series of moored barges, motor-powered to be moved in winter. According to legend, Feng Hou, one of the six ministers of the Yellow Emperor, was killed in combat here and a tomb was erected in his honour. △

Three Gates Gorge (Sanmenxia)

When the Yellow River turns east near Tongguan it enters the Yuxi ravine, in the middle of which lies Three Gates Gorge, one of the most dangerous parts of the waterway. Here, two rocky islands called God Gate (Shenmen) and Demon Gate (Guimen) stand in the middle of the river, cutting its waters into three channels. Of the three, the God Gate is deepest and Demon Gate most dangerous. In the Tang dynasty another waterway was cut north of the three channels to by-pass the dangers of Three Gates Gorge, but the scheme failed: when the river was low the channel was not navigable, and at high-water it became as treacherous as the main flow. A path was eventually cut along the wall of a cliff to get around the torrent, and it can still be seen above Three Gates Gorge today. △

Yellow River at Mang Mountain

After Three Gates Gorge and some 130 kilometres of ravines, the Yellow River widens again as it flows past Mang Mountain, also called Bei Mang Mountain, which lies north of Luoyang and extends to Zhengzhou as part of the Qinling Range. The region is noted for its wealth of ancient tombs — a poem by Wang Jian of the Tang dynasty tells how "Mang Mountain has very little land to spare/It is cluttered up with old graves of Luoyang people." Another writer, Zhang Ji, put a more morbid air to it: "North of Luoyang lies the road to Mang Mountain," he wrote. "Funeral carts rattle their way in the autumn air."

From a high point on Mang Mountain, the river can be seen passing under two steel bridges. Terraced croplands along its banks testify that Mang Mountain is a place of life and industry as well as death. ▽

Down River

The Yellow River sweeps to the northeast after passing Kaifeng and Lankau Counties and rushes over China's northern plains. It gets narrower and narrower until it reaches Dongping and Yanggu, where it is only one or two kilometres wide. After traversing the North China Plain, the river joins the Dawen River and continues to flow northeast. Dongping features a lake which is the only natural lake on the river's lower reaches. After Changqing the river arrives in Jinan, capital of Shandong, the last great city in the Yellow River Basin, and from there it flows through a delta covering 2,400 square kilometres and into the Bo Sea. For all its majesty and intermittent wrath, the Yellow River flows through great distances of arid and semi-arid land, and is affected by drought. The quantity of water that it carries annually to the sea is only 480,000,000 million cubic metres — one-twelfth the volume of the region's other great river, the Yangtze. △

Sunrise over the Yellow Mountain, Anhui Province

The Central Region (South)

This region covers seven provinces, includes an immense basin that was once a lake, is linked by the main waters and tributary system of the nation's mightiest river — and, in many respects, can be called both the physical and emotional heartland of China. Its main artery is the Yangtze River, 6,300 kilometres long and the world's third biggest river after the Amazon and Nile. Its complicated spiderwork of waterways knits together a territory which encompasses the warm, temperate or semi-tropical provinces of Sichuan, Hubei, Hunan, Jiangxi, Anhui, Jiangsu and Zhejiang; all of which are rich agricultural areas producing most of the country's staple and "cash" crops such as rice, cotton, silk, tobacco, peanuts, soyabeans and the so-called "lusty leaf", tea, which in only three centuries or so has become the world's leading stimulative beverage.

With such an abundance of water — the Yangtze's network and most of China's 370 large lakes — the region also produces vast quantities of freshwater fish; and the Zhoushan Archipelago off Zhejiang Province reaches into China's richest offshore fishing ground. Just south of the Yangtze Delta, where the huge river meets the East China Sea, lies Shanghai, China's late-developing centre of industry, notoriety and intellect and, with 11 million people, a metropolis now ranking in population with Greater Los Angeles.

Aside from the Yangtze, the region is dominated by the Sichuan Basin, once a mammoth prehistoric lake that was drained many millions of years ago by the rise of the earth's crust. High mountains surround this basin, the Qionglai Range to the west, Wu Mountains on the east, Daba Mountains to the North and to the south the Dalou Mountains which form part of the Yunnan-Guizhou Plateau. In its northern reaches the basin rises to form the Chengdu Plain, named for its principal city, historic Chengdu, and also called the "land of abundance". The eastern area of the basin is warm, wet and misty, with the city of Chongqing shrouded in fog for 170 days or so a year. On the lower reaches of the Yangtze, the great river, in conjunction with the Han River, has transformed what was once a sprawling marshland into a lake district and a series of four plains in which the waters and the soil are so fertile that it is known as the "land of fish and rice".

The entire region is noted for its natural and in many areas dramatic beauty, its landscape ranging from deep gorges carved through the hills by the Yangtze, "seas" of bamboo in the highlands around Sichuan, three famous sacred Buddhist mountains — Emei in Sichuan, Jiuhua in Anhui and Putao in Zhejiang — the Province of a Thousand Lakes, Hubei, and the Huang (Yellow) Mountain in southern Anhui which are renowned for their forests of pines, dramatic rock formations, "cloud seas" and hot springs.

As the heartland of China, this region has held the key throughout history to the domination of the entire empire. Its wealth was the ultimate target of constant tribal military pressure from the north. Since the Eastern Jin dynasty (AD 317-420) when the Chinese capital was moved to Nanjing, and when the later Song emperors were forced to move south, the region has been China's cultural centre and most coveted economic prize — the scene of great battles and power struggles and famous cities that were first established and developed as long as 3,000 years ago.

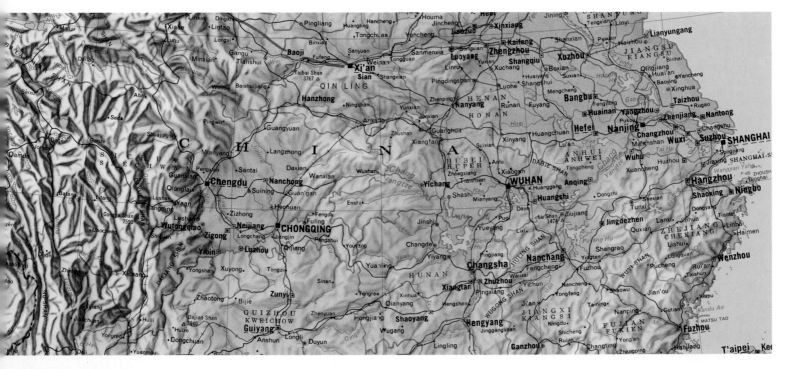

Dadu River

This, the biggest tributary of the Min River, rises out of the Guoluo Mountains between Sichuan and Qinghai and compares with the Yangtze in its potential for hydroelectric power. On its 900 kilometre course its level falls no less than 3,000 metres, and by the time it reaches the Min at Leshan its waters flow at a rapid speed. The world's largest stone Buddha image, which stands on the slope of Mount Lingyun overlooking the river, is believed to have been set up in the hope that its powers would tame the river's fury.

▽

Jiuzhai Gully

Surrounded by snow-capped mountains, this beauty spot in Nanping County on the border of Sichuan and Gansu features dense forests, a total of 108 high-mountain lakes and one of China's most dramatic waterfalls. Its name refers to nine local villages, all inhabited by Tibetans. The lakes are so clear that on a fine, still day the rocky beds and underwater vegetation can clearly be seen — giving them the names "Five-coloured Lakes", "Peacock Lake" and "Five-flower Sea". ◁

The Great Jiuzhai Waterfall

Tumbling and dashing down a natural flight of stone steps, the Great Waterfall (Dapuba) of Jiuzhai cascades 20 metres down to the floor of the gully. Not surprisingly the local Tibetans have given the falls and their surrounding wooded lakes the name "fairyland". △

Yellow Dragon Monastery (Huanglongsi)

Close to the Jiuzhai Gully, in an area of "stair lakes" (*tihu*) at the foot of the snow-capped Xuebaoding, north of Songpan County in Sichuan, is Yellow Dragon Monastery, built in the Ming dynasty. The monastery was given its name, in turn, from a legend in which the Emperor Yu travelled the country some 4,000 years ago attempting to find ways of controlling a great flood, and was aided by a yellow dragon.

The lakes, which lie on different levels of the terraced slope, are formed by the waters of melting snows and are noted for the iridescence of their waters, caused by refracted sunlight.

The area is also noted for military expeditions which passed through its forests and lakes in legend and in recorded history. Some of the great generals of the Warring States (475-221 BC) are said to have marched their armies through there, and it is recorded that the Tang dynasty general Hou camped there on a march north to suppress the Xiongnu and other nomad Tubo tribes. Not much is left of the Yellow Dragon Monastery — only a

rear building — but a festival there each year attracts pilgrims from as far as the arid plains of Gansu and Qinghai. ▷▷

Home of the Giant Panda

Jiuzhai Gully, abundant with bamboo, is also a main habitat of the giant panda, China's most unique and most endangered native animal and symbol of the World Wildlife Fund. In the summer the pandas move up into the cooler mountain areas, where Tibetan tribespeople operate ingenious bamboo watermills in a rustic form of hydro-electric power. In the winter, the "bear-cats" as the Chinese call them return to the valleys and are known to scavenge village gardens and rubbish dumps for food. ◁

Dujiang Dam

This huge engineering project and its quaint ancient suspension bridge stand where a famous dam known as the "fish mouth" was built in the 3rd century BC to control the floodwaters of the Min River west of Guan County in Sichuan. Early records hailed the dam as a marvel, because "there is no fear of famine (in) this well-watered land." It removed the annual suffering from floods and helped turn Sichuan into one of the richest agricultural areas in China.   △ ▷

Two Princes Temple

Standing on the east bank of the Min River, this temple was originally built in tribute to a prince of the period of the Northern and Southern dynasties, which existed after the fall of the Han monarchs. But in AD 497 it was re-dedicated to Li Bing, the prefect of Shu County, and his son for building the vital Dujiang Dam. Its bamboo suspension bridge (opposite page) has been known by several names over the centuries but is now popularly known as "Husband-Wife Bridge", in honour of another family partnership responsible for its reconstruction nearly 200 years ago. Each year thousands of people from all over Sichuan gather at the temple and slaughter sheep to celebrate the anniversary of the birthday of Li Bing's son.   ◁▽

203

Qingcheng Mountain

This mountain, with its 36 peaks and 72 caves, is typical of the quiet beauty of much of the Sichuan area, and attracts many tourists. Lying southwest of Guan County, it features two sacred landmarks, the Tianshi and Shangqing Temples. The Tianshi (Teacher from Heaven) Temple was built in the Sui dynasty and its main hall houses a statue of Shen Nung, reputed to be the father of Chinese agriculture. Built in the Jin dynasty, the Shangqing Temple features a portrait of Laotze who lived around 590 BC and founded Taoism, the native religion based on harmony between man and nature. Both temples were renovated in the late Qing dynasty.

▽▷

The Great Buddha of Leshan

Looming 71 metres high, with enough room on its crown to accommodate over 100 people, this is the largest stone Buddha image in the world. In the Tang dynasty it was located in a thriving community of Buddhist monasteries, carved into the western wall of Mount Lingyun, southeast of Leshan in Sichuan Province. It took more than 90 years to construct and is believed to have been begun in the year 713 by a monk who hoped to tame the sweeping currents of the confluence of three rivers — the Dadu, the Min and the Qingyi. The Buddha was completed under the supervision of government officials in 803.

It was once colourfully painted and gilded with gold leaf, and a 13-storey pavilion, or "Buddha House", protected it from the weather. The structure was destroyed in the late Ming dynasty, and the statue has been exposed — much to its cost — ever since. △

Emei Mountain

Soaring 3,100 metres into the clouds in Emei County, Sichuan, this mountain was a sacred Taoist centre as early as the East Han dynasty (AD 25-220) but its temples were taken over and re-dedicated in the spread of Buddhism. Since the Tang dynasty it has been one of the four great Buddhist mountains of China. Several hundred monasteries were scattered around its lower slopes in its heyday, but now only a few remain, the most significant ones being Baoguo at the foot of the mountain, Wannian on its middle slope and Jinding at its summit. The Song dynasty poet Fan Chengda wrote of Emei Mountain:

"The Great Emei stretches its arms in friendly welcome,
While Little Emei and Middle Emei beckon in joy.
Peerless they are in charm and elegance;
No need to cross the seas for the Land of Immortals." ▷▷

Qingyin Pavilion

A black boulder shaped like an ox-heart looms over the summit of Niuxin (Ox-Heart) Range and the Qingyin (Sonorous Sound) Pavilion on Mount Emei in the county of the same name in Sichuan. The rock and the pavilion mark the confluence of two other Sichuan rivers, the Bailong (White Dragon) and Heilong (Black Dragon).

▷

Wannian Monastery

East of the main peak of Emei Mountain, and below Double Dragon Mountain, only three of the original seven buildings of this Jin dynasty monastery still stand. And those that are still there were renovated in the reign of the Ming ruler Wanli. The monastery possesses rare Buddhist sutras written on the leaves of the bei-duoluo tree, and a 62-tonne bronze sculpture of a Bodhisattva riding a six-tusked elephant.

◁

Dragon Gate Gorge of Daning River

Called Wuxi in ancient times, the Daning River rises on a mountain slope on the border of Sichuan, Shaanxi and Hubei Provinces and flows over 200 kilometres north to south to join the Yangtze at the entrance to Wu Gorge. The landscape through which it has carved its course is so precipitous and startling that it is called the "Marvel of Gorge Country". As the river meanders south it passes through seven dramatic gorges. The most renowned are the so-called Little Three Gorges comprising the Dragon Gate (Longmen), Double Dragon (Shuanglong) and Dripping Green (Dicui) Gorges, stretching about 50 kilometres over the lower reaches of the river.

Longmen Gorge, also known as Luomen Gorge, is situated on the east of Wushan county. Going upstream from Wushan one would come to it before meeting the other two. The entrance to this three-kilometre gorge is guarded by two towering precipices like a gate; hence its name. △

Dripping Green (Dicui) Gorge

This is one of the Daning River gorges, a 20 kilometre-long stretch of sheer rock-faces which tower hundreds of metres high and are known as "Sky-Scraping Red Cliff". There are, in fact, many other colours besides red in the rock — jade-green, purple and blue, crimson and brown, silver, orange and yellow. The rock-walls lie so close together, and the river's course bends at such acute angles, that there is another gorge called Guanmenyan, or Closing Door Cliff, which appears to have no access at all until a boat virtually reaches its rock-face. Then, a narrow passage appears, only to "close" again when the boat is through. Around the gorge, lush vegetation has all but covered an ancient tribal stronghold called Luojiazhai, and there are weirdly shaped stalagmites and stalactites and a waterfall with such a fine curtain of spray that it is known as "Flying Rain from the Heavenly Spring". ▽

Double Dragon Gorge

This gorge, along with its sisters — Dripping Green and Dragon Gate — is on the lower reaches of the Daning River, close to its meeting point with the Yangtze. The system of gorges is about 10 kilometres long, and its sides are so high in some places that low-lying clouds become trapped between the faces, creating an atmosphere of mystery and fantasy. Stalactite caves and strange rock formations enhance this atmosphere, conjuring up dramatic visions enriched by local lore. There is a winding ridge called the Dragon's Entry, and a cave characterised by a brown rock crossed with black veins called the Tiger's Exit, while four huge stalactites resembling two stallions burrowing their way head-first into the rockface are referred to as Horses Drilling through the Hills. △

Stone Sculptures at Dazu

These hill carvings, started in the late Tang dynasty and completed over a period of 250 years, cover no less than 45 sites in Dazu County. They were first commissioned by Weijing, the governor of Changzhou, around AD 892 and the work was carried on through the Five Dynasties and Northern Song periods and into the reign of the Song emperor, Xiaozong. The Tang sculptures (below) are among the finest, reflecting the sophistication and refinement of that age, and include Bodhisattvas with rosaries and upraised palms and accompanying dragons and other beasts, birds, landscapes, pavi-

lions and mansions. It is ironic that, in an age in which Buddhist art achieved such distinction, the religion should have come under the hammer of imperial disapproval. However, when the relatively brief period of suppression ended, the invention of block-printing enabled scholars to publish a vast bibliography of Buddhist translations and the religion enjoyed new popularity and growth.　▽

Buddhist Sculptures at Baoding Mountain

This horseshoe-shaped hillside tableau, northeast of Dazu County in Sichuan, was started in the Southern Song dynasty and took from 1133 to 1162 to complete. Later sculptures were added during the Ming and Qing reigns. Today, the statues, engravings and bas-relief images — more than 15,000 of them — rank with the grottoes at Mogao and Dunhuang in the legacy of early Chinese Buddhist art. Most of the sculptures refer to Buddhist stories and include the Six Paths of Reincarnation, Story of the Radiant Peacock Deity, Stories of the All-encompassing Buddha and the Transforming Phases of Hell. But the most dramatic and inspiring work by far is the huge recumbent Sakyamuni Buddha (left) which attracts thousands of Buddhist pilgrims each year.　◁ △

Little Sea of Tiequ

Many snow-clad peaks dot the Miu River Basin in northern Sichuan. Beneath these mountains, in the river valley, are numerous tranquil lakes. As these lakes lie in huge terraced shelves in the hillsides, water flows down from an upper lake in the form of cascades.

This high-altitude lake, known as the Little Sea of Tiequ, like others in the area, was formed by debris deposited by glaciers and volcanic eruptions. The rich underwater plantlife gives the lakes their dark green colour; their waters, however, are crystal clear. △

212

Du Fu's Cottage

The bard Du Fu, who lived in the years AD 712-770 in the Tang dynasty, is regarded as one of the two greatest poets that China has ever produced. He was beloved for his sympathy for the poor and downtrodden victims of injustice and the almost constant casualties of Chinese history, those of internecine warfare. During the violent insurrection led by An Lushan against the hopelessly infatuated Emperor Xuanzong, Du Fu took refuge for four years in this small home on the western edge of Chengdu, and managed to turn out about 240 poems. The cottage was rebuilt as a shrine in his name during the Northern Song dynasty, and its present design is the result of further renovation in the years 1500 and 1811. A statue of the great writer stands in an exhibition hall that was added to the home in the Qing dynasty. There is also a Qing tribute in the main study that reads:

"Let us contemplate the dearth of poets of great stature through the centuries.

Here lived one whose cottage will last as long as the land exists."

▽▷

Hall of the Three Sus

This magnificent estate and residential complex in Sichuan's Meishan County stands on the site of the home of the celebrated Song dynasty literary family of Su Xun and his two sons Su Shi and Su Zhe. Though all three men were noted bards and scholars, Su Shi (better known nowadays as Su Dongpo) became one of the dynasty's most famous poets — and governor of Hangzhou in 1089-1091 — and there are memorials and tributes to him in various spots in Sichuan and Guangdong Provinces. A memorial hall was added to the family estate in the Ming dynasty but was destroyed. It was rebuilt in 1665 and re-developed in 1928 and named the Three Sus' Park. This Great Hall (Qixian) features some of the literary works of Su Shi and his relatives, along with stele rubbings of their calligraphy. △

Zhang Fei Temple

Thought to have first been built 1,700 years ago and renovated several times since, this temple on the south bank of the Yangtze in Sichuan's Yunyang County features a wealth of Song dynasty calligraphy and other artwork. Among its treasures are a poem by Su Shi (Dongpo) on the Red Cliff (a battle field that saw the defeat of Cao Cao of the Three Kingdoms period in AD 208), and the Rhapsodic Essay on Orchids by Huang Tingjian. A stele rubbing, also on show, commemorates the famous Petition to Conduct a Punitive Expedition (Chushibiao) in the cursive script of the Song general Yue Fei. ◁

White King City (Baidicheng)

Before the time of the Western Han dynasty, Baidi Mountain on the northern bank of the Yangtze in Sichuan was known as Fish Belly County (Yufu Xian). According to legend there was a well there which gave off a white mist in the shape of a dragon. The warlord Gongsun Shu, who was in control of the area, saw this as a propitious omen and in AD 25 declared himself the "White King" and built a fortification on the hill. After his death 12 years later a hall was built in his memory, and it was renamed White King Temple in the much later Qing dynasty. The story of the White King has captured the imagination of many poets, including Du Fu, whose lines "Clouds wander out of the City of the White King/And rain pours down on the White King City" are among the most well-known. The poet Bai Juyi had this vision:

"On Jutang Gorge's gate, the mist hangs low; On White King City's wall, the moon looks to the west."

△

Green Cliff Mountain (Qingyan Shan)

Green Cliff Mountain, noted for its picturesque or bizarre rock formations, is a group of 2,000 mountain peaks at the junction of three counties in Hunan Province. Legend and imagination have given the peaks various names, such as Golden Whip Boulder in memory of an incident in which the first emperor of Qin is said to have lost a whip there. Other peaks are known as Three Sisters, Rooster Cliff, or Monkeys-Storming-Heavenly-Palace Peak, depending on their shapes.

Huilong Bridge

This beautiful covered bridge is typical of the architecture of the Dong people, a tribal ethnic minority living on the borders of Guizhou, Hunan and Guangxi Provinces.

The bridge spans a stream in Tongdao County, western Hunan, and was probably built as late as the Qing dynasty. It is 80 metres long, four metres wide and constructed entirely of pine, with all parts dovetailed so that there is not one nail in the entire structure. The bridge consists of two sections. The western section rests on several layers of beams which were placed one above the other to cantilever out on both ends and form a rudimentary haunch of an arch to distribute the weight of the bridge above to the pier below. The eastern section rests on beams which in turn are supported by wooden blocks that sit on the brick pier. The

Double Phoenix Pavilion (Shuangfengting)

This green-tiled structure with its ornate triple-eaved six-cornered roof was built in memory of the philosopher brothers Cheng Hao and Cheng Yi who lived in the time of the Northern Song. It stands on Lutai Hill in Huangpi County in Hubei. According to legend, shortly before both brothers were born their mother had a dream in which two phoenixes appeared and entered her bosom, and this later inspired the pavilion's name. Their father, the mayor of the county, was mentioned in Song dynasty records as being "benevolent but strict", and he encouraged the two boys to be scholars. The present pavilion is not the original one; it was built in 1848, succeeding several others which had been erected on the site over the centuries. The Cheng brothers themselves are mentioned in historical records as aspiring to be great sages while in their teens and eventually mastering the philosophies of Confucius and Mencius.

▽

covering is a double-eaved, wooden-tiled roof which the Dong call a "wind-and-rain" structure, somewhat similar to the covered bridges of the North American snow-belt.

The Dong tribe number fewer than one million and are mostly farmers and foresters, and yet they are among the most artistic people in China. Their women are skilled weavers and the brocades they produce are intricately patterned and long-wearing. The Dong people are also noted for their folk theatre and their invention of the *liukong* (six-hole) and *shuchui* wind instruments.

◁ △

Shennongjia

Originally the site of an old glacier, this mountain range overlooks the Yangtze River between Hubei, Shaanxi and Sichuan Provinces, and covers an area of 3,200 square metres. The highest peak, rising to over 3,000 metres, is called the Roof of Central China. The name Shennongjia is derived from the story of Shennong, mythical father of herbal medicine who "tasted the myriad herbs" for their medicinal qualities. Shennong is believed to have built a lodge on this mountain range, distilled the Elixir of Life there, and then turned into an immortal — whereupon the lodge became a forest. The region is in fact rich in plantlife. More than 2,000 species grow on the slopes, including

rare medicinal herbs such as ginseng, angelica sinensis, gastrodia elata and eucommia. The habitat of over 500 species of wildlife, it is the home of bears, South China tigers, "gold coin" leopards, deer, flying squirrels, wolves, pandas and monkeys. In recent years, strange unidentified five-toed footprints half a metre long have been sighted — so far the largest footprints in the world to be recorded. ◁ ▷

Swallows Nest (Yanziya)

This mountainous area 35 kilometres northeast of Shennongjia is almost constantly enveloped in clouds and mist, so much so that it is known as the mountain that "never sees summer". It is also constantly raining there, so the vegetation is naturally lush. The mountain wall also features a huge cavern called Swallows Cave which includes an opening section big enough for a thousand people to gather in and an inner sanctum in which thousands of swallows nest all year round. A rare bird called *wogehui* ("My brother, come back") inhabits the slopes, named after a legend in which a maiden mourned the loss of her brother so bitterly that she transformed into a bird of that name. ◁

Bronze Statue of Zhenwu

The regal, corpulent 10-tonne statue of Zhenwu rests in the Golden Hall of Wudang Mountain in the province of Hubei. It is flanked with statues of the traditional servants, Golden Boy and Jade Girl, and attended by two bodyguards, the Fire General and Water General, both in the act of drawing their swords. Built in 1416, the Golden Hall lies on the summit of Wudang's Sky Pillar Hill. ▽

Wudang Mountain

Otherwise known as Taihe Mountain, Wudang includes 72 peaks and 36 cliffs and covers an area of 400 square kilometres in Jun County, Hubei. It also has so many scenic spots — caves, springs, pools, terraces and fountains — that Mi Fu, the great calligrapher of the Song dynasty, gave it the reputation, still alive today, of being the "Prime Mountain of China". The mountain is a sacred place in Taoism, the religion based on harmony with nature, and many Taoist disciples in ancient times came here to perfect their disciplines, including Zhang Sanfeng of the Ming period who introduced a style of martial art called "Wudang boxing". In the Ming dynasty some 300,000 people were recruited to build a Taoist monastery here that included 72 cliff temples.　　◁▷

Zixiao Temple

Built in the Yuan dynasty in 1413, this temple northeast of Wudang Mountain's Sky Pillar Peak has a main hall featuring an august and dignified statue of the Jade Emperor, the supreme master of the Taoist gods. Also known as the Pearly Emperor, Yu Huang, the Jade Ruler is one of three supreme deities, the Pure Ones, of Taoism. It is believed that he was borrowed from the Buddhist hierarchy, the Buddhists adapting him in turn from Brahma, the almighty creator of Hinduism. Whatever, he stands majestically in the Zixiao Temple's principal hall surrounded by statues of his attendant gods. This temple is one of the finest on Wudang Mountain and is designed to harmonise so ingeniously with the craggy terrain that its buildings create a novel "exposing and hiding" effect in which some seem to appear while others disappear as visitors walk along a mountain path leading to the complex. Other buildings in the temple are the Dragon and Tiger Hall (Longhudian) containing sculptures of both beasts and a Stele Pavilion featuring two three metre-high stone sculptures of tortoises.　　◁

Jade Fountain Mountain (Yuquan Shan)

Shaped like an upturned boat and also named Overturned Boat Mountain (Fuchuan Shan), this softly contoured hill lies 15 kilometres west of Dangyang County in Hubei. It is often shrouded in mist and is thickly vegetated with more than 400 species of plants and trees, including the spectacular pigeon tree which, when in bloom, looks as though a flock of pigeons is roosting in it. The mountain also features a gingko tree which is said to have been planted in the Tang dynasty over 1,000 years ago. The area is also famous for its tea, which the great tea connoisseur, Lu Yu, who wrote the 8th century *Cha Jing*, or *Tea Classic*, ranked as the second finest in China. On the hill's eastern slope there is a monastery and a Pearl Fountain where General Guan Yu of the Three Kingdoms period (AD 221-263) is said in legend to have passed on his horse, both man and steed extremely thirsty. His horse struck the ground with its hoof, so the story goes, and water gushed out "like a string of pearls". ▷

Jade Fountain Monastery

This monastery, on the eastern slope of Jade Fountain Mountain, was built between AD 196 and 219 and for a long time was recognised as one of the four paramount woodland monasteries in China. In 1021 it was expanded to include nine mansions, 18 halls and living quarters for 3,700 monks and priests, and so became one of the region's largest places of worship. Seven main buildings still stand, along with cedar trees that are said to have been planted in the Ming dynasty and a garden in which hangs a huge iron wok engraved with the inscription "cast in the 11th year of the reign of Daye

of Sui with 3,000 catties of iron". It testifies to the wealth and power of the monastery in those days, but on a terraced mound to the east of the complex there is an even more remarkable testimonial — a pagoda cast entirely of iron. ◁

Jade Fountain Iron Pagoda

It took 53 tonnes of iron to cast this astonishing pagoda in sections in 1061, the structure rising 18 metres high with 13 storeys, each embellished with cast decorative panels and bas-reliefs. It is literally covered with "double dragon playing with a pearl" motifs, Buddha images and niches housing engraved Buddha deities, some of them riding lions or elephants. At one time a big wind-bell hung from one of the eaves, and its sonorous toll could be heard several kilometres away. ▷

Qu Yuan Temple

This imposing temple with its red-pillar façade was erected in memory of Qu Yuan, who, in 278 BC, threw himself into the Miluo River in grief at the defeat of his state of Chu in the Warring States struggle. At the rear is a mound where he is believed to have written his famous "Li Sao" ("The Sorrow of Parting"). His suicide has since been commemorated by the annual Dragon Boat Festival. During the boat races people throw rice into the waters, reenacting a gesture in which rice and other food were thrown where he drowned to keep fish and turtles away from his body. ▷

Kaiyuan Temple

This similarly imposing place of worship was built in the reign of Emperor Xuanzong of the Tang dynasty. Legend has it that one night a giant appeared in the emperor's dreams and said, "I want to stay. Please build me a temple." Soon after this, an iron statue of a god came to light. The emperor lost no time in ordering the temple's construction. △

Liu Yi Well

This well, with its sculptured gods and fish, is situated on Zhongjun Hill on Dongting Lake. It was named after the scholar Liu Yi. Liu is said to have met a girl here who claimed to be the daughter of the Dragon King of the lake and complained that she was being cruelly treated by her husband. According to folklore Liu informed her father and when the story reached her uncle he promptly killed the bully. ▷

Lake Dongting

Lying in the northern reaches of Hunan Province and covering an area of 2,800 square kilometres, Lake Dongting is the second biggest freshwater lake in China. Its name means "Cave Home of Immortals", and therefore it has always been a sacred spot. Its nearby Jun Hill was once packed with 48 temples and 36 pavilions, but most of them were destroyed over the centuries by fire or civil strife. Only a handful remain, including Two Concubines Tomb, and Wine Fragrance Pavilion. The lake has 11 towns dotted around it in an area which produces cereals, fish, lotus products and tea. Another noted product is two rare species of bamboo, Luohan and Xiang Concubine, named after the concubine buried there. ▽

Yueyang Mansion

This majestic building stands at the western gate of Yueyang City in Hunan on a site which has a history going back to the Han dynasty. It is said that in the period of the Three Kingdoms, which followed the Han rule, one of the warring generals, Lu Su, used it as his command post. The mansion itself was first built by Zhang Shuo in the Tang dynasty, and it became an inspiration for several noted poets. In the Song period the mansion was renovated and the poet Fan Zhongyan was invited to write about it. He came up with his celebrated "Yueyanglouji" in which the keynote were these somewhat existentialist lines:

"To feel concerned before the world feels concerned;
To enjoy only after the world has started enjoying."

The present mansion is the result of another extensive renovation in 1880, and the building — along with its splendid tilework (below) — has since been compared with the famous and recently restored Yellow Crane Mansion of Wuchang, and Tengwang Mansion in Nanchang. ◁ ▽

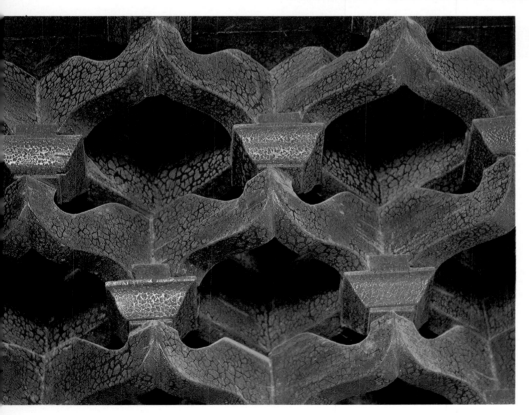

Aiwan Pavilion

The Aiwan Pavilion stands in an idyllic setting on a hillside slope above the Qingfeng Gorge in Yuelu Mountain, Hunan. It was probably built in the reign of Qianlong (1736-1795) and has certainly been renovated since the turn of this century. It stands in an area of maple trees, and in the autumn when the leaves turn golden and red it is one of the most popular and romantic scenic spots in the region. It was previously known as Red Leaves Pavilion and Lovely Maple Pavilion. A couplet inscribed in stone at the entrance begins:

"The hilly paths are aflame with red leaves like peaches..." △

Heng Mountain

Known as South Sacred Mountain in ancient times, Heng Mountain and its 72 peaks run for a distance of several hundred kilometres through the middle of Hunan Province. Its tallest peak, Zhurong, reaches 1,290 metres and is a favourite spot for viewing the sunrise. Naturally, it has also been a favourite haunt of poets, including the Song dynasty bard Huang Tingjian who, standing on Zhurong's summit, saw "Looking up, the myriad stars I strain to touch/Looking down, the dusty world is far, far away." ▽▷

Nanyue Great Temple

This palatial Great Temple of South Sacred Mountain stands on a site first developed in the Tang dynasty in Nanyue Town at the foot of Hunan's Heng Mountain. Its main hall was rebuilt in 1882. It consists of nine main buildings including two halls, pavilions, a library and the imposing Kuixing Mansion (above); and the structure of the main hall includes 72 pillars representing the 72 peaks of the southern range. A circular stone balustrade around the hall is decorated with 144 marble panels carved with landscapes, birds, beasts, flowers and insects. Much of the complex is in the architectural styles of the Song and Ming dynasties, reflecting the renovation and extensions that have taken place since the Tang

reign. A large iron bell was installed in the temple in the Yuan period, and the poet Li Bai wrote a tribute to Heng Mountain that was inscribed in the later age of the Ming on a stele and can be studied there today. △

Green Shadow Wall (Luyingbi)

Built over 500 years ago, this Green Shadow Wall of alum shale bricks is typical of Taoist shadow walls built throughout China before the gates of official buildings to deflect evil spirits and other "noxious influences". Sometimes an enormous red sun was depicted on the walls to reflect the pure and bright principle of yang and encourage civil servants to observe diligence and justice. The Luyingbi stands at the gate of a palatial Ming dynasty mansion complex in Xiangyang City in Hubei. In 1858 the mansion was destroyed in the Taiping Rebellion, but the wall survived. Ninety-nine dragons are carved on the wall, and once played with a pearl "bright as the sun" which referred to the legend of what is believed to have been a solar eclipse in Xiangyang. The pearl is now missing. △

Guqin Terrace

This beautiful terrace and hall, enclosed in a white marble balustrade, lies beside the Moon Lake in Hanyang, Hubei. Its name means Ancient Zither Terrace, and it was first built in the Northern Song dynasty nearly 1,000 years ago to commemorate the deep friendship of a *qin* (zither) master, Yu Boya, and a recluse named Zhong Ziqi of the Spring and Autumn Period of 770-476 BC. Their love and understanding of each other, and music, was so strong that when Zhong died the zither maestro destroyed his instrument, vowing never to play again. The term *zhiyin* (music understood) has since been synonymous with true friendship.

△ ◁

East Lake

Covering 33 square kilometres, East Lake lies to the east of Wuchang and has so many inlets and curves around its bank that it is also known as the "lake with no limit". It is surrounded by six scenic and historic spots that are called Tingtao (Listening to the Waves), Mo (Mill) Hill, Luoyan (Descending Wild Duck), Baima (White Horse), Chuidi (Playing the Pipe) and Luohong (Gem). The Tingtao section features an island and a three-storey mansion called Hangyinge (Strolling Chanting Mansion) with a statue of the poet Qu Yuan — its name referring to a line in his epic "Sorrow of Departing" that tells of "Strolling by the marsh,

chanting." Nearby is the Nine Women Pier commemorating women martyrs who died in battle against the Manchu Qing forces in the 1858 Taiping Rebellion. Other spots feature monasteries and monuments going back to the Tang and Song dynasties, and even further back to the time of the state of Wu. ▷

Site of the Military Regime

A bronze statue of Dr Sun Yatsen, the founder of the 1912 Chinese republic which replaced some 3,000 years of dynastic rule, stands at the gate of this former government headquarters in Wuchang. Before the republican revolution the buildings and their central watchtower were used as a training base for the Qing imperial cavalry. When the Qing dynasty was toppled in 1911 it became the temporary headquarters of the republican provisional government. ◁

Gulongzhong

This is the place where the strategy of a "divided" China, separating the country into three distinct states, was formulated prior to the Three Kingdoms Period of AD 220-280. It was also where Zhuge Liang, the brilliant political and military tactician of the state of Shu, is said to have spent 10 years as a recluse in a cottage before being persuaded to serve as prime minister to the Prince of Shu. ▷

Yanshui Pavilion

Standing in the middle of Gantang Lake in Jiujiang City, Jiangxi, this pavilion is relatively new — built with funds raised by a monk named Gu Huai in the latter part of the Qing dynasty. But the history of the site is considerable. It goes back to the raising of an army in the Three Kingdoms Period more than 1,700 years ago, and is where two pavilions were built in the Tang dynasty and the reign of the Northern Song, only to be demolished by 1522. In the Ming reign another pavilion was erected there, but eventually met the same fate — pulled down in 1853. ◁

Hundred Flowers Islets (Baihua Zhou)

Hundred Flowers is the name of three small islands in the East Lake, one of which features the striking red-pillared pavilion pictured to the right. In this pavilion there is an inscription of a couplet composed of lines from two different poems, Bai Juyi's "Song of the Pipa" and the "Pavilion of Prince Teng" by Wang Bo:

"Where reeds and maples rustle in the autumn wind;
The lakes are cold and pellucid, the days are peaceful."

Between AD 1131 and 1162 in the Song dynasty, the islands were used as a training centre for a force of what would now be called "water commandos". Later it was given a more peaceable role: Su Yunqing of the Song era retired here to spend his last days in quiet harmony in what became known as the Garden of the Venerable Su. ▷

Gantang Lake

Fed by streams from Lu Mountain, this lake in the centre of Jiujiang City was originally called South Gate Lake and features a long dike with an elegant balustrade built in the Tang dynasty. It leads to the Yanshui Pavilion, erected in the time of the Song. From here, visitors can climb to a panoramic viewpoint at Yingyue Mansion. Elsewhere the lake features an old monastery and pagoda, along with the Suo (Lock) River Mansion and Langjing (Wave Well) whose name comes from a saying that goes: "When the Long River (Yangtze) heaves with waves, even the wells respond with ripples." ◁

Lu Mountain

This, one of China's most delightful mountains, rears to the south of Jiujiang City and overlooks the Yangtze River. Its name *Lu* means lodge, and legend says it was where seven brothers named Kuang built a lodge in the time of the Zhou dynasty (1050-221 BC). Legend also has it that the great healer, Dong Feng, one of the noted mountain shamans of early Chinese history, made his home at the foot of the mountain. He is said to have refused payment for his services and usually asked his patients to plant five apricot trees when they recovered. In the time of the Eastern Han dynasty (AD 25-220) more than 380 monasteries existed on the mountain's slopes, a few of which still stand after centuries of care and renovation. Lu Mountain's "sea of clouds" is a celebrated tourist attraction, as are its many peaks, caves, pools and waterfalls.

Home of Badashanren

This splendid white-walled former monastery in Nanchang, Jiangxi, was taken over in 1661 by the painter Chu Da, better known as Badashanren, a descendant of Ming royalty who sought refuge from the newly installed Manchu Qings. Called upon to serve his new masters, he feigned madness. He also kept himself inebriated to avoid being done away with under suspicion of conspiring against his Qing masters. For all that, Chu Da managed to continue painting and is highly regarded for the economy of his brush-strokes in ink painting. His influence on Chinese art has been considerable, and his style is much admired and imitated by traditional artists even today. ▽

Shiqiao Yan

Originally called Qi Mountain, this 600 metre-high hill southwest of Baiyueling in Xiuning County, Anhui, is crowned with a natural stone "bridge". Its arch frames a nearby peaked outcrop of rock. Mountains, especially those with significant natural formations such as this, featured in nature worship, the earliest form of religion in China. Around 2000 BC the Emperor Shun decreed that the mountain should appear among 12 symbols known as the Twelve Ornaments embroidered on the robes of state of all court officials. Mountains, he told them, symbolised the constancy and firmness which all rulers and their ministers required — though only the emperor himself had the right to display all 12 emblems; mountains and dragons were handed down to the second level of hereditary nobles. △

Apricot Blossom Village (Xinghuacun)

This lake in the western district of Guichi County in Anhui was the site of Apricot Blossom Village, famous for its wines in the Tang dynasty. It is mentioned in a poem by Du Mu, along with the product of its famous Huanggong distillery:

"It is grave-sweeping time, and an unceasing drizzle reigns
Adding sadness to filial worshippers on the roads.
'Pray, where is the nearest winehouse, cow-herd boy.'
'In the Apricot Blossom Village.' "

Thanks to the exceptionally clear water of its wells, the district still produces wine, notably Peach Blossom Village Daqu Wine, which is exported far and wide and has kept alive the district's historic reputation. △

Judge Bao Temple

Judge Bao, also known as Xi Ren, lived in the Northern Song reign and was noted for his incorruptibility and steadfast refusal to bend to official pressure. People called him "Bao Qing-tian" ("Bao Blue Sky") because of the clear, unclouded quality of his character. The temple in his name was built in the Ming dynasty on a small island in the River Bao in Hefei County, Anhui. It features, among other things, a well called Incorruptible Fountain whose waters are said to give any blemished drinker a tell-tale headache. ◁

Taibai Mansion

This three-storey mansion with its flamboyant flying eaves was first built between AD 806 and 820 in memory of one of the two greatest poets of China, Li Bai (701-762). Aside from his works, he is renowned for having tried to "catch the moon" (or its reflection) in a river after a number of drinks and almost drowning. The mansion stands in Caishiji, southeast of Ma'anshan County in Anhui, and its present design follows renovation that was carried out at the end of the 19th century. A large screen facing the main gate bears a painting of Li Bai on a visit to Caishiji, and in the shrine itself there are two wooden sculptures of the famous bard. ▽

Jiaonu Terrace

Aside from including one of the most beautiful and best-preserved monasteries in Anhui Province, Jiaonu Terrace has a history that goes back to the East Han dynasty of AD 25-220. It is said that Chief Minister Cao Cao built Jiaonu Terrace as a training ground for a force of 500 archers to prepare for an attack by one of his two main rivals, Sun Quan, the warlord of the state of Wu in southeast China.

The monastery stands on the terrace, originally called Iron Buddha Monastery. First built in the fifth century, it was renamed Ming Jiao Yuan and then Ming Jiao Si. There is here a six-metre-high iron Buddha weighing six metric tons. The monastery was rebuilt in 1870 and a new Da Hong Bao Dian (Hall) was built in 1886. The main entrance has steps leading to the terrace. A gate stands there with single eave half-hipped, half gabled roof. The Da Hong Bao Dian is double-eaved with half-hipped, half-gabled roof, covered with cylindrical tiles and devoid of brackets. The monastery is well shaded and possesses many stone sculptures. △▷

Nine Flowers Mountain (Jiuhua Shan)

Lying in Qingyang County of Anhui, this craggy mountain area took its name from a poem by the Tang dynasty bard Li Bai. It has also been recognised for centuries as the "Citadel of the Buddhist Empire". As long ago as AD 401 a Buddhist monk built himself a meditation retreat here, and at the advent of the Tang dynasty the king of Xinluo began erecting other places of worship. During the Song and Ming dynasties, and into the Qing reign, so many institutions were added that at one point the hills contained more than 400 monasteries for more than 4,000 monks and nuns. Just over 70 of those places have survived, along with a rich legacy of about 1,500 Buddha images and valuable paintings and murals and ancient sutra prints. The range covers 100 square kilometres and includes 99 peaks, the tallest, Shiwang (right), rising to 1,342 metres. ▷

Gubaijing Terrace

This Tang dynasty monastery, rebuilt in the reign of the Qing emperors, perches on a terrace under the sheer face of Jiuhua's Tiantai Peak and is said to have been the place where Bodhisattva Kitigarba paid homage to the sutra in the year AD 653. An engraved footprint of the distinguished visitor is still on display there. This patron saint of Jiuhua is worshipped as a ruler of the Buddhist nether world, and his task is freeing suffering souls from purgatory. He is also protector of infants. ◁

Yunfang Rock in East Cliff

A huge boulder, 20 metres long and 10 metres high, shaped like an ancient pleasure boat, dominates East Cliff in the centre of Jiuhua Mountain — along with an elegant bell-pavilion which was once part of the East Cliff Monastery. East Cliff was named by the poet Wang Shouren who was banished there by the Ming court and spent his remaining days in contented solitude spending "the whole day watching the falling flowers/Not being aware of the whereabouts of home." The Youming bell in the pavilion still rings, filling the valleys with its deep chime.
▷

Qiyuan Monastery

The monastery took its name from the garden where Sakyamuni resided when he lived in this world. One of the four great surviving monasteries of Jiuhua Mountain, this building very nearly crumbled into ruin within years of its construction some time after 1522 in the Ming reign. With no resident abbot to maintain it, the monastery was in a state of disrepair when the Zen master Longshan stepped in and saved it. It soon became a flourishing Zen centre, attracting great numbers of worshippers each year, and when Longshan died it passed into the hands of two of his disciples.

The monastery has an unusual asymmetrical layout. Its principal architectural feature is the striking gold glazed tiles. The front hall features a carving of a three-eyed god brandishing a whip and an inscription that warns:

"With three eyes to oversee the world's affairs, With a lash to give warning to all people."

Inside the rear hall there are three gilded Buddhas, each six to seven metres tall, sitting on lotus pedestals (right). These are the largest Buddha images in the Jiuhua Range. They are flanked by the 18 arhats, each sculpted with a different facial expression. The walls behind these images are decorated with colourful murals depicting stories from the Buddhist scriptures, and adding solemnity to the decor of this big hall.

△▷

Chess Board Rock (Jipanshi)

Aside from its monasteries, Jiuhua Mountain is also famous for its evocative rock formations, formed by wind and rain erosion on granite outcrops. Chess Board Rock is one of the strangest of them — even the veins of the rock on its face criss-cross to form the pattern of a chess board. Other noted sights in the mountain range are Douji (Fighting Cocks), Sanfu (Three Axes), Feilai (Arriving by Flying), Hutou (Tiger Head), Huachuang (Flower Window) and Dingxin (Steady Heart).

▷

Yellow Mountain (Huang Shan)

Legend has it that the Yellow Emperor once tried to distil the Elixir of Life on this magnificent mountain between She and Taiping Counties in Anhui. A Pailou (entrance arch) announces the area, the beauty of which has been celebrated for centuries, the great Ming dynasty traveller Xu Xiake paying it the warmest of all tributes when he wrote: "Having returned from the Five Sacred Mountains, one does not want to look at ordinary mountains; having returned from Yellow Mountain, one does not want to look at the Five Sacred Mountains."

Yellow Mountain's main peaks all rise over 1,800 metres and the area is noted for its forests of pines, two lakes, three waterfalls, 24 streams, 72 peaks, its hot springs and its "sea of clouds".

▽

Shixinfeng

This dramatic mist-shrouded peak on the eastern side of Yellow Mountain, rising to 1,600 metres, has rightly been described as the embodiment of all traditional Chinese landscape paint-ing. Toward its sharp summit there is a stone-slab bridge called Ferrying Immortal's Bridge, named after a nearby pine that has grown through a crack in a boulder and looks like someone carrying an Immortal across a stream.

▷

Yuping Peak

Rearing in petrified waves towards the sky, Yuping (Jade Screen) Peak is another dramatic aspect of the Yellow Mountain area. It looms between Lian-hua (Lotus Blossom) and Tiandu (Heavenly Capital) Peaks and is close to the range's hot springs. It also features the Yuping Lodge, a well-positioned resting place for the weary climber, which is said to stand where a monk, Pumen, dreamt of the Bodhisattva Manjusri in the year 1614 and erected a shrine to commemorate the vision. Standing 1680 metres above sea level, the entire peak is granite, and obviously thrown up by some cataclysmic eruption hundreds of millions of years ago. This explains why both the ascent and descent are treacherous. Ways are steep, and one of the most

dangerous points is the Xiao Xin Po (Be Careful Slope), which has a sheer wall on one side and overlooks a deep ravine on the other. Nearby lies the pretty, high-altitude Yuping Sky Lake.

▽

Ciguang Monastery

In the early days of Buddhism in China, with the threat of official persecution, civil strife or common banditry always present, most monasteries were built with isolation and security in mind. Some of them, especially in the mountains along the dangerous Silk Road, were so ingeniously sited that travellers could pass within a hundred metres of them and never know they were there. Ciguang Monastery, nestling below Yellow Mountain's Zhusha Peak, could be reached only by way of a steep and quite perilous footpath in the old days, and the Ming dynasty traveller and scholar Xu Xiake recorded how he had to virtually climb trees and rocks to get there. The monastery has a long history, but today is remembered only as the place where two illustrious Qing painters, Shih Tao and the monk Huangren, took up temporary residence.

△

Xuanwu Lake

Xuan means "dark" and refers to a legend in which a black dragon once appeared on this small four-square kilometre lake in the eastern district of Nanjing. Its waters were once used to train water commandos, and at one time in the Song dynasty it was drained and turned into farmland. It was filled with water again in the Yuan reign and made part of a public park shortly after the turn of this century. Five small islands dot the lake, all of them featuring popular viewpoints (Cherry Blossoms, Trees-in-Clouds, Misty Willows, etc) along with a tomb-shrine built in memory of Guopu of the Jin dynasty.
▽

Zhongshan Mausoleum

This, the mausoleum of Sun Yatsen, the father of republican China, was built between 1926 and 1929 on the southern slope of Mao Mountain, east of Nanjing in Jiangsu Province. Facing south, the layout follows that of traditional Chinese tombs, a sacred arch and avenue (this one stepped) leading to a main gate, stele pavilion, podium, tomb hall and then the grave chamber. The entire mausoleum is set in some 80,000 square metres of forest and gardens. Dr Sun Yatsen was born in 1866 in Guangdong Province and for years was an activist seeking to reform or overthrow the hidebound Manchu Qing dynasty — but, like Russia's Lenin, was forced to spend much of his time outside China in England, the USA, Europe and Japan. He returned from exile in 1911 to claim victory and set up a provisional republican government after a successful uprising by urban workers supported by dissident units of the Qing army.
△

Mochou Lake

This small lake just outside Shuiximen, Nanjing, was part of the Yangtze River in the 5th century and is believed to have been sealed off and beautified during the Tang reign. Certainly, by the middle of the 14th century the first emperor of Ming, the former monk Zhu Yuanzhang, built a mansion here called "Win Chess" for the many epic struggles he had there with one of his generals, Xu Da. It is said that in one particular match the general cleverly managed to arrange his pieces so that they formed the characters "Wansui" ("Long Life"). The emperor was so impressed that he presented him with the mansion as a gift. The lake's name comes from a folk story about a girl from Luoyang who became a great benefactor of the poor, and a white marble statue of her stands in the mansion grounds (right). ▷

Narrow West Lake (Shouxihu)

Five beautiful yellow-glazed tiled pavilions stand on a 15-arched bridge in Narrow West Lake in Yangzhou, Jiangsu province, built by a salt merchant in 1757 to commemorate a visit by the Qing emperor Qianlong. It is also called Lotus Blossom Bridge because it was built on a bed of lotus plants, and for many years it has been a popular spot for one of the favourite traditional pastimes of the Chinese, viewing the moon and its reflection on still waters. The White Pagoda stands within the nearby Lianxing Monastery and is a copy of the White Pagoda in Beijing's Beihai Park. It is said that the salt merchant had it built in one single night to impress the visiting emperor — a story that is taken with a grain of salt.

△

Sheli Pagoda of Qixia Monastery

Located behind the Qixia Monastery northeast of Nanjing, this pagoda is said to be where Emperor Wen of the Sui dynasty, founded in AD 581, kept the Sheli (Sarira) cremation remains of the Buddha. He is said to have built it in 601, and it was renovated three centuries later by two chief ministers of the Tang court. The

pagoda features eight carved panels depicting the life of Sakyamuni from his descent from heaven: entering the womb, development in the womb, birth, earthly travels, enlightenment, preaching, defeating demons and final transition to Nirvana. ▷

Wangshiyuan

Suzhou (Soochow) has for centuries been known as one of central China's most beautiful cities and the place where wealthy mandarins, merchants and landowners built fine retirement residences, many of them connected to the network of lakes and canals that have given the city the reputation of being the "Venice of the East". Wangshiyuan, a particularly well designed and opulent home, was built by Shi Zhengzhi of the Song dynasty and named "Ten Thousand Volumes Hall". In 1736 it was bought by Song Zongyuan, who changed its name to "Fisherman Recluse" and chose Wangshi (Master of the Net) as the name of its garden. With its cottages, pavilions, studios and ponds it embodies all that the wealthy retired required of life — visual pleasure and harmony. △

Zhuozheng Garden

Another famous Suzhou residence, the Zhuozheng (Simple Life) Garden, was built in 1513 by a retired civil servant, Wang Xianchen, on the site of the former Dahong Monastery. He took its name from a poem on leisurely living by Pan Yue of the Jin dynasty, a line from which goes: "To water the garden and grow vegetables is a form of government by the simple soul." Renovated in the Qing reign, this is now the largest and most splendid residential garden in Suzhou. Since its first occupant, it has had some illustrious owner-residents, including the grandfather of the novelist Cao Xueqin (*Dream of the Red Mansion*) and Li Xiucheng, a leader of the Taiping Rebellion against Manchu rule. ▽

West Garden (Xiyuan)

This palatial residential complex and garden in Liuyuan Street, Suzhou, has a colourful and complicated history. First built between 1522 and 1566 by a retired Ming dynasty mandarin, it was then converted to a monastery by his son; then, in the 19th century, demolished and rebuilt in its present form. It still includes the monastery, and a main hall that houses the images of 500 arhats and a statue of the monk Ji Gong whose face, viewed from the right, has an amused, happy expression, but from the left is sad. Viewed from the front it appears to be happy and sad all at once. The pond that links the various buildings is well-stocked with colourful carp, and is home to a tortoise that is said to be 300 years old. △

Jinshan (Gold Hill) Monastery

This elegant monastery in Zhenjiang City in Jiangsu, was first built in the Eastern Jin dynasty (AD 317-420). During the later Tang rule, gold was discovered there and the monastery's name was changed to Gold Hill. Its dominant pagoda was first erected as one of twin structures in the Song dynasty. One was later destroyed, and the present pagoda is the result of reconstruction in 1900. Among the monastery's valued relics are the "Four Treasures of Jinshan", a bronze tripod of the Zhou dynasty (770-221 BC), a battle drum said to have been used by the Shu Han tactician Zhuge Liang in the Three Kingdoms conflict, a Song dynasty jade belt of Su Dongpo and a painting by the Ming dynasty artist Wen Zhengming. △

Tai Lake

The Tai Lake is the third biggest freshwater lake in China and is famous for its rocks — strange and somewhat bizarre natural formations which have been used all over China to decorate parks and gardens. It is also where Fan Li, the mastermind who helped the Prince of Yue to inflict vengeance on the Prince of Wu in 476 BC, is said to have celebrated his victory by taking the most coveted beauty of that time, Xi Shi, for a boat ride. The lake covers 2,400 square kilometres and spreads into the provinces of Jiangsu and Zhejiang. It is fed by two streams, the Tai and Jing, and empties through four others into the Yangtze. There are 48 small islands in its waters and the peaks of 72 hills parade around it. ◁

Baodai Bridge

The Baodai (Precious Belt) Bridge, seven kilometres southeast of Suzhou, is believed to have been given its name when the prefect of Suzhou sold his precious belt to raise funds toward the cost of its construction in AD 806. It is thought to have been built first of wood, then rebuilt with stone in 1232. Just over 600 years later, it was rebuilt and took the design that it features today. The bridge is 317 metres long and has 53 arches, three of them large enough to allow junks or river launches and barges through. When the full moon is reflected on the water under each of the arches it is said to look like a string of 53 moons, or a belt of bright jade. △

The Tiger Hill (Huqiu) Pagoda

Built in the middle of the 10th century on Tiger Hill in Suzhou, this eight-sided seven-tiered tapering pagoda is constructed of bricks but in the style of traditional wooden structures. In 700 years from the 12th to 19th centuries it suffered seven major fires that badly damaged the top and all the eaves. What remains now is the basic brick structure, which requires constant maintenance. First named the Yunyan Pagoda, it is probably the oldest of its design south of the Yangtze River. It stands 50 metres high and every floor is accessible by a wooden staircase.

On every storey, there are murals of peonies. Other features, such as the cantilevered brackets and coffered ceilings, are also painted over with rather special designs. ◁

Hanshan (Cold Mountain) Monastery

Cold Mountain Monastery in Fengqiao, Suzhou, dates back to AD 502-519 but was destroyed by fire several times over the centuries and its present structure goes back only to the beginning of this century. Its name is said to have come from the monk Hanshan, who came to the area with a colleague, Shide. Gilded statues of both men are housed in its great hall. The Tang dynasty poet Zhang Ji immortalised the monastery in lines that spoke of "the sound of the midnight bell (coming) to my lonely boat". The bell disappeared a long time ago, and a replacement installed in the Ming dynasty has also gone — it is now in a collection in Japan. A new one hangs in Hanshan, made in Japan and donated to the monastery. ▷

261

Yandang Mountain

Yandang Mountain is situated in Leqing County, Zhejiang. The leading peak, Yanhugang (Wild Goose Lake Peak), lies 1,046 metres above sea level. It was so named because wild geese reside in the lake on the peak where reeds and rushes flourish.

The igneous rocks give the mountain its rugged appearance and a tint of red. The mountain has been a favourite of poets and painters, providing them with inspiration for poems, paintings and travels. Some of the artists who visited the mountain include Xie Lingyun the poet, Shen Kuo the Song dynasty scholar, Tang Yin the painter and Xu Xiake the veteran traveller of the Ming dynasty. Its popularity is not surprising, since the towering fortress-like peaks and cliffs embrace more than 360 scenic spots. The sheer faces have also provided sanctuary and safety for Buddhism, and there are many ruins of old monasteries among its peaks.   △

Liuhe Pagoda

The Liuhe Pagoda, also known as Six Harmonies Pagoda, stands on the Qiantang River in Hangzhou and was first erected in AD 970 in the belief that it would help placate mischievous spirits and control local flooding. The present brick pagoda was built in 1153 and its wooden eaves were renovated in 1899. The octagonal pagoda is nearly 60 metres high, with 104 iron wind-bells playing from the corners of its eaves.   ▷

Lingyin Monastery

This famous monastery stands to the northwest of the West Lake in Hangzhou. Its site was selected in AD 326 (Eastern Jin dynasty) by the Indian abbot Huili, who decided it was a fitting "hermitage for the Immortals". During the Five Dynasties following the collapse of Han rule, the devoutly Buddhist Zian Liu, the prince of Yue, greatly expanded the monastery to include nine mansions, 18 pavilions and 3,000 monks and novices. When the Qing emperor Kangxi visited the huge complex on his trip to southern China, he gave it the name Cloud Forest Zen Monastery (Yunlin Chansi). The monastery still features its ornate Great Hall (opposite, lower picture), a 33.6-metre high structure which houses a 9.1-metre tall gilded statue of Sakyamuni Buddha (above) sitting on a lotus pedestal, based on a well-known sculpture of the Tang dynasty. A lengthy couplet describing famous scenic spots in Hangzhou is inscribed on two tall pillars in front of the statue. The hall is also decked with other images and paintings representing Buddhist mythology, and two ancient stone plaques with inscriptions from the scriptures. △▷

Feilai Peak Stone Carvings

This sculpture of the Maitreya in the form of the Laughing Buddha is among 300 stone carvings that adorn the walls and caves of Feilai (Flown Here) Peak near the Lingyin Monastery. Its name comes from the monastery's founder, the Indian monk Huili, who is said to have commented on a visit there: "This looks like a hill of the Immortal Vulture Mountain of Tianzhu. I wonder when it flew and settled here." The sculptures were begun in the Five Dynasties period (AD 907-960) and added to in the reigns of the Song and Mongol Yuan.

◁

Grave of Yue Fei

General Yue Fei, the Song dynasty military chief who was wrongly accused and put to death by his political rival, Qin Hui, was originally buried on Hangzhou's North Hill, but his tomb was moved to Qixia Hill beside the West Lake in 1163. Near the entrance to the tomb there stands a pavilion called Zhongbai (Loyal Cedar) housing a petrified cedar tree. It is said to have suddenly died when the general was executed. Nearby is the Temple of General Yue, which was once known as Zhonglie (Loyal Martyr) Temple. The present building is the result of renovation in the Qing dynasty. ◁

Temple of General Yue

Two rows of red lacquered pillars lead to the main hall of the Temple of General Yue, each engraved with scenes of his most famous Song dynasty battles against Jin invaders. Another engraving displays the characters "Xinzhaotianri" (Heart as Clear as Sun in Sky), based on the general's last words before execution. The seated statue of the great warrior was only recently cast and installed. Over it hangs a plaque inscribed with four Chinese characters "Huanwoheshan" (Restore to Us Our Land and Rivers) and the ceiling is painted with more than 370 white cranes, symbolising loftiness and staunch loyalty. ◁▽

West Lake of Hangzhou

The West Lake was called Golden Cow Lake before the Song dynasty because a golden cow was said to materialise on its waters whenever a sage or holy man passed by. Later, the poet Su Shi (Dongpo) compared the lake with the famous beauty Xi Shi, writing that, like the courtesan "it is attractive with make-up or without". The lake site used to be a shallow bay connected to the Qiantang River, but was gradually sealed off by alluvial deposit, and dredging and landscaping did the rest.

This oval-shaped lake has an area of about six square kilometres and a circumference of 15 kilometres. The average depth of the lake is about 1.5 metres, with the deepest part being only 2.8 metres and the shallowest spot less than one metre.

The city of Hangzhou stands on its eastern shore. On the gentle slopes of the hills surrounding the three sides of the lake are large gardens displaying a variety of flora: peach blossom in spring, lily in summer, osmanthus in autumn and plum blossom in winter.

The hills are dotted with pavilions, pagodas, grottoes, mansions and streams.

The lake also adds its beauty and mystique to the Ten Beautiful Sights of Hangzhou — Autumn Moon over the Smooth Lake, Spring Dawn over the Su Bridge, Snow over the Broken Bridge, Dusk at the Thunder Peak Pagoda, Evening Bell from Nanping, Waving Lotuses on a Garden Pond, Golden Carp in Huagang, Listening to the Nightingales under Willows on Lakeside, Moon Reflected on the Three Ponds and Double Peaks Piercing the Clouds.

Apart from being a scenic spot, the lake supplies water for irrigation and is rich in aquatic products.   △

East Lake of Shaoxing

This lake, along with the West Lake of Hangzhou and the South Lake of Jiaxing, are together known as the three great lakes of eastern Zhejiang. Its long dyke was built during the final Qing dynastic reign to separate its waters from those of the Grand Canal. Bridges and pavilions were also erected and the lakeside beautified with peach and willow trees. Nine stone bridges span the lake, dividing it into three sections. On its shores there are two caves which have for many years been popular tourist spots — Xiantao (Immortal Peach) and Taogong Caves, both of which can be reached by boat. A stone column at Immortal Peach Cave is inscribed with a couplet that says the "cave is deeper than five hundred feet/The peach trees blossom every three thousand years" — a gross exaggeration, but a nice one. ◁

Putuo Mountain

Taking its name from a Sanskrit term meaning "beautiful white flower", Putuo Mountain lies on an island-county of the same name to the east of Zhoushan archipelago. Legend has it that the goddess Guanyin appeared here once, and since then it has been one of the four great Buddhist mountain retreats of China. A group of precariously balanced boulders proclaim the mountain's importance in big red characters that read "Sea-Sky-Buddha Kingdom".

It is said that in AD 916 a Japanese monk set off from Wutai Mountain to carry an image of Guanyin back to his country. When he reached Putuo Mountain he was caught in the winds of a typhoon, so he built a monastery there dedicated to "Guanyin who will not leave". This was probably the first of the many monasteries built on Putuo Mountain. In 1214 an edict was issued

ordering that Guanyin should be the principal object of worship there. In its heyday Putuo Mountain had more than 300 monasteries, temples and shrines. Pu Ji, Fa Yu and Hui Ji Monasteries are the three most renowned monastic buildings. Pu Ji Monastery is the principal monastery devoted to the worship of Guanyin. Hui Ji Monastery was greatly expanded in 1907 upon the acquisition of a set of the Tripitaka sutra.

The ' monastic architecture set against the ever-changing seascape is best described by Wang Anshih of the Song Dynasty: "Lightly the clouds saunter over the hills on the sea. Here is a world away from the mundane world."

The Yangtze River

Also known as the Changjiang, or Long River, the Yangtze begins its 6,300 kilometre surge to the distant East China Sea as the trickling runoff of melting snows in the Tanggula Mountains in western Qinghai. As it gathers its immense volume it traverses Tibet, Yunnan, Sichuan, Hubei, Hunan, Jiangxi, Anhui and Jiangsu, carving itself deeply into the terrain, collecting over 700 tributaries, and draining a basin of nearly two million square kilometres — almost 20 percent of China's total land space.

The river can be divided into three main sections. The upper section ends at Yibin in Sichuan. This stretch measures about 3,500 metres. At Yibin, the Jinshajiang joins the Miujiang to become the Changjiang.

The middle section takes a zigzag course and runs for about 1,000 metres, cutting through the Sichuan Basin and the gorges of the hilly terrain of Hubei. The Three Gorges of the Yangtze are found in this section where the water reaches savage speed.

The lower section is much wider and more slow-moving. However, there are a series of sharp turns and twists in the gorges between Hubei and Hunan called the Nine Curved Intestine. Many lakes are also located in this section, the largest being Dongting, a natural reservoir of the Yangtze.

The river is probably the most important communication link in China, joining east and west and the northern provinces with those of the south. Its fertile basin supports about 300 million people, just under a third of China's total population. More than 80,000 kilometres of its main waterways and tributaries are navigable. Ships of more than 10,000 tonnes can go up as far as Nanjing and smaller vessels to Hankou, Chongqing and Yibin. If the Yellow River to the north is associated with the birth and early settlement of China, the Yangtze and its vast basin became the vital strategic prize without which no conqueror or ruler could ever hold sway over China for long.

The Yangtze is not only a huge river, third largest in the world after the Amazon and Nile, it is also one of the fiercest and most powerful.

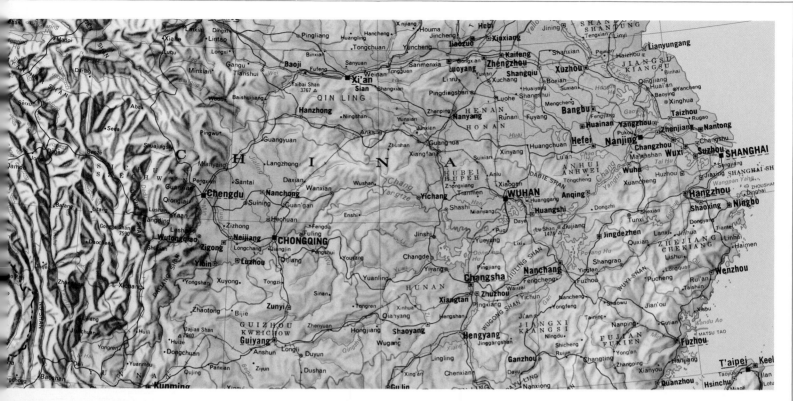

Tuotuo River

If one adopts the principle that the source of a river should be traced to its remotest spot, then the source of the Yangtze is the snow-fed Tuotuo River, 5,000 to 6,000 metres up in the Tanggula Mountain Range of Qinghai. The Tuotuo flows northward initially and after passing through a valley it crashes through the Heman Rapids, then broadens out over wide pebbled beds before reaching Hulu Lake and deflecting eastwards and widening again. The mighty Yangtze has begun. Before the Ming dynasty it was thought the Min River fed the Yangtze, but it is now commonly recognised that this high-mountain runoff is in fact the source.

▽

The Middle Section of the Yangtze

The Yangtze swells until it spreads 800 metres wide and as much as 35 metres deep as it reaches Chongqing in Sichuan Province. Here, its power is also strengthened by a major tributary, the Jialing, which joins it near the city. Chongqing is often referred to by the single-character name Yu, which in fact was its name until Emperor Guang-zong, the Prince Gong of Yu, ascended to the throne and decided to celebrate by changing it. Its present name translates into Double Joy.

It also takes a name Shangceng (Hilly City) from the hills and slopes on which it is built. The picture above shows the Yangtze near Chongqing at sunset. △

Shibaozhai

Shaped like a Chinese jade seal, with hanging cliffs on all four sides, the hill on which Shibaozhai stands is called Jade Seal Hill. Rising abruptly from the bank of the Yangtze between Zhong and Wan Counties in Sichuan, this hill affords yet another scenic spot on the river's middle course. Shibaozhai is the name of the remarkable struc-

ture that crowns this hill. Essentially a fort, it consists of a gate located on the bank of the river, a 12-storey tower leading from the gate to the hill-top, and a monastery which stands at the top. The entire structure measures 60 metres in height, and is built into the contours of the hill in wood and stone. Constructed during the reign of the Qing emperor Kangxi (1662-1723), it boasts many stone plaques with famous inscriptions. ▽▷

Baidi Hill

This broad terraced hill, lying in the eastern part of Sichuan's Fengjie County, is where the Yangtze flows into 193 kilometres of deep gorges and jagged rapids. Because of its position it has always been of great strategic value, and many battles have been fought for control of it over the centuries. Beyond Baidi Hill, the Yangtze hits the Jutang Gorges, down which the Tang dynasty poet Li Bai took a hair-raising ride, describing how "On both sides of the river the gibbons cry incessantly/As the light skiff speeds past hills on hills." △

Shennufeng

This former glacier, one of the 12 peaks of Wu Mountains, stands on the north bank of the Wu Gorge overlooking the the Yangtze in Sichuan's Wushan County. Its name means "Goddess" and it is said that from a distance it looks like a girl standing in a graceful pose. It is also called Wangxia Peak, or Looking at Coloured Clouds, because it is the tallest in the area and therefore is the first to catch the sunrise and the last to reflect the setting sun.

In ancient Chinese mythology, the daughter of Xiwangmu, the Heavenly Mother, is said to have descended from heaven to help the ancient ruler Yu, who was charged with the mission of controlling the great deluge that was sweeping over all of China. After giving him written instructions on the methods he should employ, she decided to remain on earth and dwell on this peak, and was later buried on the southern slope of Wu Mountain. Many poetic works depicted her as a fairy beauty involved in romance with mortal beings, and a temple is devoted to her worship in the county town nearby. ▷

Jutang Gorge

This, the shortest of the so-called Three Gorges of the Yangtze, is also the most dramatic. Its mouth is very narrow, less than 100 metres across, with steep walls on both sides, and the Tang dynasty poet Du Fu described it aptly when he wrote of it as the gate through which all the waters of Sichuan battle to gain access. Another poet, Bai Juyi, came up with this description: "The banks are like two screens kept ajar, through which the sky peeks." Yet another bard, un-named, created an even more rhapsodic vision: "The tops of the cliffs touch the sky; the boat seems to navigate underground." Guarding the mouth of the gorge are two mountains — Tuzi Mountain (Pear Mountain) on the left and Bai Yan Mountain (White Salt Mountain) on the right.

Two iron poles are embedded in the rock on both sides of the gorge, and are said to have been put there by Zhang Wu in the year AD 904. According to records of the Five Dynasties era, Zhang installed iron chains between the poles to regulate traffic on the river. The idea behind this was defence, but in later periods the barrier was used to extract tolls from passing river tradesmen.

On the cliff of Bai Yan Mountain a series of holes drilled through the rock runs in a zigzag line down from the peak until it reaches the foot of the

mountain. These are the remains of the wooden footpath used by the ancient herb collectors.

In a steep wall on the north bank, there are a number of neatly carved rectangular caves which are believed to have contained the remains of nobles of the Warring States period. Nine "hanging coffins" have been found, containing human bones and bronze swords. The tiny tombs are similar to those of the Toraja mountain tribe in South Sulawesi, Indonesia, who not only buried their nobles in specially cut niches in cliffs but also installed life-like, fully clothed wooden effigies of them. △

Xiling Gorge

Spanning a distance of 70 kilometres between Sichuan and Hubei Provinces, the Xiling Gorge is the longest of the three and it is also the most dangerous. There are not only narrow passages bristling with half-submerged rocks but a series of severe rapids too, including the perilous Kongling Rapids which a local folk-song has described as the "demon's gate". The stretch of white water is risky enough when the level of the river is low and its rocks are exposed like jagged teeth, but when the Yangtze is swollen and they are submerged they are an even greater danger to the hulls of river craft. ▷

Wu Gorge

Wu Gorge is the most picturesque of the Three Gorges of the Yangtze, a scenic picture gallery cutting more than 40 kilometres through the main ridge of Wu Mountain. Xu Rulong of the Qin dynasty waxed enthusiastic about the scene, writing "As I put out my boat in the Wu Gorge my heart is with the twelve peaks" — referring to the 12 mountain summits that range around the narrow waterway. In the 'Song of the Three Gorges' the Song dynasty poet Lu You spoke of how "over the bow of my boat a green splendour fills the autumn air". Other literary tributes ranged from the peaks "floating in the purple void" to "precariously hanging in the blue vault". Beneath one parti- cular peak, Jixian (Gathering Im- mortals) the scene is described with crushing simplicity in an inscription that reads "Multiple-Cliffs-and-Piled-Up-Hills Wu Gorge". △

Yangtze Estuary

After entering Jiangsu Province the Yangtze bends to the northeast around Ningzhen in a sweeping semicircle. Beyond that the land is low-lying and flat, less than 10 metres above sea-level. At last, the Yangtze has ended its 6,300 kilometre journey to the sea, emptying through the vast 50,000 square kilometre Yangtze Delta. Thirty million years ago the delta was a triangular bay dotted with islands, but since then the Yangtze has dumped so much mud and debris into it that it is now a plain and the islands are mounds and small hills. The force of the river, especially in flood time, continues to change its banks, and its alluvial deposits have actually pushed the coastline out to sea at the rate of one kilometre every 40 years. South of Chongming Island the Yangtze is joined by another of its tributaries, the Huangpu, as it finally pours into the East China Sea. On its south bank stands the nation's most cosmopolitan trading and industrial city, Shanghai. ◁

The karst hills of Guilin reflect in the placid waters of the Li River, Guangxi Province

The Southern Region

The southern region of China, covering the provinces of Yunnan, Guizhou, Guangdong, Guangxi and Fujian, is not noted for its role in the vanguard of Chinese history. Yet it was one of the first areas of China to trade with the outside world and was the scene of a bitter 19th century struggle with the "foreign devil" that ultimately brought the age-old dynastic tradition to an end. It was the power-struggle in the so-called Opium War of 1839-42, centred on the thriving trading concession at Guangzhou (Canton) that saw the British Navy defeat China's imperial war-junks, grab the island of Hong Kong and a slice of mainland territory as a colony and open the way for an international "carve-up" of Chinese sovereignty that the weakened, antiquated Manchu Qing dynasty could not effectively resist.

Physically the region is divided into the highlands of Yunnan and Guizhou and the lowland areas of the other provinces. These in turn are dotted with abrupt, weirdly shaped towers and cones of limestone, giving Guilin in particular its unique and long-renowned beauty and poets and painters a fountainhead of inspiration. Fast-flowing rivers crisscross the region, gouging deep gorges in the karst terrain — as deep as 3,000 metres in the highland areas — and the landscape also features huge caves, underground rivers, "stone forests" and red sandstone terraces. The climate ranges from sub-tropical to tropical and is influenced along the coastal areas by both the monsoon and the dreaded typhoon — powerful hurricane-force anticyclones that boil up out of the Pacific south of the Philippines and surge north to dash themselves, one after the other, on the south China coast.

Though not very outstanding historically, the region is noted for the discovery in Yunnan of the oldest known bronze drum, dating from the 5th century BC. One of China's great irrigation systems was built in Guangxi during the short but crucial Qin reign (221-207 BC). There are monuments in Yunnan — the Three Pagodas of Daji, Stone Bell Hill and the monasteries of Chicken Feet Mountain — that are a legacy of the province's political importance between the 8th and 13th centuries. The Guangxiao Monastery in Guangdong Province dates back to the 3rd century BC. Perhaps the greatest of the region's legacies, however, is the role it played for centuries as a refuge for scholar-mandarins who had lost favour in the imperial courts.

The region is also famous for being the flashpoint of rebellion, the last and greatest of these being the republican campaign against the Manchus led by the sons and daughters of southern merchants and officials who, like the region itself, had become more modernised and therefore more progressive in thought than China's northern areas through contact with foreign traders, teachers and missionaries.

Diqing White Reservoir

This long, narrow terraced valley floor lies between snow-capped mountain peaks in the Yunnan highlands, and is typical of the "wild beauty" of much of the southern region — largely the result of water erosion on the karst or limestone terrain. Clear streams cascade down the white and pinkish steps that the waters have carved and sculptured over millions of years. Geologists believe that most of the southern region was once under water, and a tumultuous rise in the earth's crust threw up the limestone plate that covers most of the area. ▽

Tiger Jump Gorge (Hutiaoxia)

Another typical feature of the landscape in the western mountain areas of the south, this gorge cuts through hills 3,000 metres or more high northeast of Lijiang County in Yunnan. Its waters are part of the Jinsha River, and they rush, twisting and turning, for 15 kilometres through the deep valley. A large boulder stands at the narrowest point of the gorge, and it is here that the area was given its name. It is said that a tiger, pursued by hunters, saved itself in the nick of time by jumping from the boulder to the opposite bank.

▷

Black Dragon Pond (Heilongtan)

Black Dragon Pond, with its beautiful triple-eaved Fayun Pavilion and the elegant carved stone balustrade of its bridge, is thought to have existed as early as the Han dynasty. It lies near Kunming on the slope of Elephant Hill in Lijiang County, Yunnan. The pond is also called Jade Fountain because of a temple nearby, built in the time of the Ming, that goes by the name of Jade Fountain Dragon King. ◁

Shizhong Mountain Caves

The Bai tribespeople, one of several minorities scattered through the western area of the south, cut these caves in the southeast of Jianchuan County in Yunnan in the 8th century. Sixteen caves have been found, containing Buddha images and carvings depicting Bai court life — and sculptures of foreigners, demonstrating the relatively close trading communication that this region has long enjoyed with the rest of the world. △

Eight-Corner Pavilion (Bajiaoting)

Another minority tribe, the Dai, designed and built this ornate and quite unusual Buddhist pavilion in 1701 in the reign of the Qing emperor Kangxi. It stands in Menghai County, Yunnan — 15 metres high and constructed of wood and bricks. The Dai people, found mostly in the Xishuangbanna Autonomous District of southwest Yunnan, are generally Buddhist, following the lamaist school, and are noted for their ornate temples in a somewhat Burmese architectural style. Their houses are erected on stilts, leaving room underneath for the storage of boats. Like many of the hilltribe and lowland minorities of this region, they are an artistic people especially in clothing and personal ornamentation — their women wear an exotic combination of colourful turbans, silver bracelets and necklaces and other trappings and long slim ankle-length sarongs. ▽

Grand Mansion (Daguanlou)

This airy, palatial square pavilion-shaped mansion stands on an island outside Kunming city on the northern tip of Lake Dian. Aside from its splendid architecture and setting, its main feature is a famous couplet which decorates its main doors — it consists of 180 characters, 90 on each door, and is reputed to be the longest couplet ever written. The mansion was built in 1682 and was first called Buddha Temple. Two centuries later it was renovated and beautified with bridges, willows, dikes, and galleries. Lake Dian, covering an area of 340 square kilometres, is the sixth largest freshwater lake in China. △

Qiongzhu Monastery

The first Zen monastery to be built in Yunnan province, Qiongzhu lies deep in a forested area of Yu'an Hill in Kunming. Besides the usual Buddha images and other relics and artwork, the monastery features life-like sculptures of the 500 arhats, each about one metre high and arranged in a complicated tableau that Li Guangxiu and five assistants took six years to complete between 1883 and 1889. Qiongzhu (Bamboo Temple) is believed to have first been built in the Tang dynasty. At its gates stand two fir trees that are said to have been planted more than 500 years ago. ▽

Lake Dian

Otherwise known as Kunming Lake, this narrow stretch of water, 40 kilometres long and eight kilometres wide, lies southwest of the city. Its upper reaches form an area of dense reeds and rushes called West Lake, or Little Sea of Grass. The lake lies close to Kunming's West Mountains a chain of hills in the shape of a girl reclining on her side — named, not surprisingly, Sleeping Beauty Mountain. There is a legend which tells of the birth of both the lake and the mountains. A fisherman's daughter was in love with a young man who, one day, disappeared in a violent storm. She wept so much that her tears formed the lake and she herself became Sleeping Beauty Mountain.

This area was populated as long ago as the 3rd century BC, the time of the Warring States, and ancient

tombs have been excavated in the vicinity. Famous scenic spots such as the Grand Mansion and the Zhenghe Park line the shores of the lake. The region yields fish and rice, and is agriculturally very productive. ▽

Dragon Gate (Longmen)

This remarkable complex of paths and caves, cut high in the side of a sheer cliff, derived its name from the mythological tale of the ancient hero Yu who opened up Dragon Gate to curb the deluge.

In actual history, the creation of this scenic spot is no less legendary. The path and grottoes took 72 years to carve out of the rock, beginning in 1781 in the reign of the Qing emperor Qianlong. Then a sculptor named Zhu Jiage spent eight years carving various images to decorate the main cave-hall, including a statue of the god of literature. One day, a pen-brush he was shaping in the figure's hand broke off. Zhu was so mortified that he leapt from the precipice to his death. Today, the tourist threads his way up through pavilions, caves and gates until he reaches the top, an act symbolising scholarly achievement in the imperial examinations. △

The Stone Forest (Shilin)

One of the natural marvels of China, the Stone Forest in Yunnan is believed to have been formed in two stages — by the earth's crust pushing up above waters that are believed to have covered the southern region in prehistory, and then by the erosive action of wind and rain on the limestone outcrops. Under the ground, erosion by subterranean water has also created huge caves. Some of the columns rise as high as 40 metres and are linked by natural stone corridors and hanging bridges. Various spots have been given descriptive names, such as Big Stone Forest, Small Stone Forest, Long Lake, Moon Lake, Lion Hill, Layered Waterfall, and Sword Blade Pool (below), where a sword-like stone peak rises dramatically out of the water. Footpaths and pavilions have been added to guide visitors through this bizarre maze, which has been the source of many fairy legends.

Yuantong Monastery

Yuantong (Enlightenment) Monastery was constructed between 1301 and 1320 in the northeast district of Kunming. It is an ornate complex, standing on the side of a small lake and featuring an elegant triple-arched stone bridge. Pictured right is one of the monastery's main buildings, an eight-cornered pavilion, featuring a touch of the 20th century — decorative lights on its roof. The monastery lies at the foot of Yuantong Hill, the highest viewpoint in Kunming. ▷

Lingzhi Forest

This is a more recently discovered stone forest in Yunnan, found 20 kilometres northeast of Lunan County. The name Lingzhi refers to the shapes that the elements have given the karst rocks, that of a fungus called Lingzhi (glossy ganoderma). These rocks, along with the stone forest 126 kilometres southeast of Kunming, have been called the ninth wonder of the world. Some say they should be among the other eight.　　　　　◁

Terraced Fields

So much of China is hills and mountains and so huge is its population — around one billion people, a quarter of the world's total population, and all but 11 percent of them working on the land — that the demand for agricultural land is enormous. For centuries, hillsides have been terraced and cultivated for the farming of rice, tea, cotton and a variety of other agricultural produce. Yunnan Province is so short of lowland area that terraces are widely distributed in the highlands east of Ailao Mountain.

Some of these terraces are cut into slopes that rise as high as 2,000 metres. The slopes are levelled into horizontal strips, with low earthen walls lining the outer edges, thus facilitating irrigation and preventing soil erosion. Spreading out from the areas of denser population — town settlements locally known as *bazi* — these terraced fields form picturesque asymmetrical patterns in different shades of green, yellow and brown, lending colour to the landscape.　　▽

The Grass Sea

Yunnan shares the waters, and is drained by, major rivers that pass through neighbouring Vietnam, Thailand and Laos — the Salween, great Mekong and the Red and Black Rivers. In the north of the province, the border with Sichuan is formed by the upper reaches of the Yangtze — only here it is called the Jinsha or Golden Sand River. In Weining County, this river and its flats have become so overgrown with reeds, rushes and other vegetation that it is called the Grass Sea. It is a rich freshwater fishing area and a natural reserve for bird life and aquatic animals. △

Jiaxiu Mansion

This three-storey wooden mansion with three tiers of green-tiled flying eaves stands in Guiyang City, Guizhou. It was built in 1597 and is noted for its many plaques engraved with literary couplets. ▷

Flower Stream (Huaxi)

Part of the Nanming River, the Flower Stream is the centrepiece of a public park situated 17 kilometres south of the town of Guiyang. The banks of this shallow stream are renowned for their lovely scenery of ploughed fields and village settlements. In the park four hills are identified — the Unicorn, the Phoenix, the Tortoise and the Snake, each with outstanding picturesque features such as caves, cliffs, waterfalls, pavilions, bamboo groves, flower beds, bridges on streamlets and boating resorts.

The upper reaches of Flower Stream pass under a stone bridge which zigzags between the banks, following the path of a weir. Nearby, a string of 100 large stepping stones runs from one bank to the other. In the summer this is a favourite haunt for swimmers, while tourists like to climb the many towers and terraces erected along the shores.   ◁ △

Rhinoceros Cave (Xiniudong)

This vast cave in Zhenning County, Guizhou, takes its present name from fossilised rhinoceros remains found in the area in 1975. It is 400 metres deep and big enough to hold more than 1,000 people. The rhinoceros, or "sworded cow," roamed areas of Sichuan before becoming extinct. Fossils of rhino teeth, called "Dragon's Bones," are occasionally discovered and ground into a powder for the preparation of medicinal tonics. It has always been such a much sought-after ingredient of traditional Chinese medicine that it is little wonder that the species died out in China. Nowadays, rhinoceros horn is imported from Africa, Thailand, India and Sumatra, though there are various strong conservationist campaigns attempting to stop it. In olden times the horns were also used as drinking vessels, and were said to "sweat" the liquid in them if it contained poison.

▽

Yellow Fruit Tree (Huangguoshu) Waterfalls

Close to Rhinoceros Cave, this waterfall, the largest in China, spans a

width of 30-40 metres and thunders 60 metres down into Rhinoceros Pool, a cascade almost equalling the size and power of Niagara Falls on the United States-Canadian border. The waterfall derived its name from the "yellow fruit tree" (tangerine) plantations found upstream of the River Baishui, which at this point in Guizhou's Zhenning County descends the hillslopes in nine steps, this waterfall being the highest and most dramatic.

A pavilion on the opposite cliff commands a full view of the cascade, and in a stalactite cave below spectators can watch the magnificent downpour through three openings. It is claimed that the roar can be heard some five kilometres away. △

Hongfu Monastery

This pretty but relatively modest monastery stands at the summit of Qianling Mountain in Guizhou and is noted for its statues of the Sakyamuni and Maitreya Buddhas, the goddess Guanyin and Guanyu, the God of War. Emperor Guan, as he is also known, is one of China's most popular gods and is said to be a deified military hero from Shanxi Province who raised an army and suppressed a rebellion in the late Han dynasty. Later, he was taken prisoner and executed by a rival warlord, but his spirit is said to have continued to work for the protection of the nation and in 1594 he was officially declared a god. ◁

Qianling Mountain

Heavily wooded and rising over a large lake, this gentle mountain range sprawls through the northwestern area of Guizhou Province. It has many hills, the most noted of them being Elephant Hill, White Elephant Hill and Sandalwood Hill. Near the lake, the karst rock has been eroded by an underground stream to form a big cavern called Unicorn Cave. ◁

Drum Tower of East Guizhou

This exquisite but sadly dilapidated wooden building, a drum tower, is characteristic of the traditional architecture of eastern Guizhou Province, which is populated mainly by Dong clans. The Dong group themselves under surnames, and each village has a drum tower which serves as a meeting place, entertainment centre and an alarm post. A leather drum is hung from the topmost eave and used to summon village elders for urgent consultation, or to raise the entire village in the event of an outside threat. The Dong are also found in Hunan Province and in the Guangxi Zhuang Autonomous Region. ▽

Qifeng Village

Looking like a scene from a fantasy story, the village of Qifeng (Strange Peaks) lies only a few kilometres from Guilin, celebrated throughout China and known throughout most of the rest of the world for the limestone mounds, towers and cones that form its unique natural architecture. The extraordinary blend of placid, flat rice-paddies, meandering rivers, lush vegetation and the abrupt tombstone effect of the mounds has challenged poets and painters throughout China's history. One of them, Han Yu, wrote of it: "The river is a turquoise gauze belt, the mountains like a jade clasp." ◁

Fubo Hill

Rising up from the bank of the Li River in Guilin, Fubo Hill is one of the most popular hills for tourists and painters alike in the fairyland setting of the karst country. Artists of all persuasions have visited the hill over the centuries and writers have left their calling cards on it: among the tributes inscribed on the rock there is a poem by Fan Chengda and a self-portrait by the painter Mi Fu, both of them of the Song dynasty. ▽

Camel Hill

This limestone outcrop to the east of Guilin looks so remarkably like a camel that it is difficult to imagine it known by any other name. However, there is another similarity and a story to go with it. The hill is sometimes called Ewer Hill because it also has the shape of a wine ewer, and at its foot there is a spot called the Grave of Lei the Drinker — commemorating Lei Mingchun of the Ming dynasty who had a habit of climbing to the summit to drown his sorrows in wine, lamenting the collapse of the Ming. △

Elephant Trunk Hill

This is another imaginatively shaped outcrop at the confluence of Guilin's Yang and Li Rivers, and the subject of a rather sad legend. It is said that the King of Heaven, taking a tour of southern China, brought with him an elephant which fell ill in Guilin. A local farmer nursed it back to health, and in return the elephant worked for him in the fields. The Heavenly King considered this a betrayal, and put the poor creature to death. It promptly turned to stone. ▽

Yangshuo

There is a well-known saying that goes: "The rivers and hills of Guilin are the most beautiful in China, and those of Yangshuo surpass Guilin's."

Certainly, the contrast of limestone and tropical green, and the hills

and their surrounding flat paddylands, is one scenic aspect of this karst landscape. The Li River winds through the hills like a green silk ribbon. Yangshuo village itself, at the end of an 80-kilometre boat cruise from Guilin City, is one of the most picturesque centres of the area and is surrounded by karst peaks that resemble ancient Chinese hats, galloping horses, a writing brush and a five-fingered hand. All this, packed into a small town area, has inspired the following Tang dynasty saying:

"The town walls encircle less than two *li* of space, but all the houses are hidden among ten thousand hills."

To the north lies Xingping, which is reputed to have "the best of Yangshuo's landscape". There, fishing rafts criss-crossing the Li River against a dramatic backdrop of hills are a typical sight.

Reed Pipe Cave (Ludiyan)

This magnificent cavern, packed with bizarre rock formations and stalactites and stalagmites, is in the slope of Guangming Mountain, six kilometres north of Guilin City.

It was first discovered in antiquity, and inscriptions have been found on its walls dating back at least 1,000 years. But somehow, probably because of civil war, it was forgotten for some time and then rediscovered — some say the local people kept it a secret, using it as a convenient hiding place in times of war. Ludiyan measures 240 metres across and is divided into two sections separated by a pond forming a natural barrier.

The cave features a rock called the Old Scholar, named after a sage who is said to have been so enchanted by Guilin's scenery that he began a poem about it — but, unable to conjure up words adequate enough to finish it, he turned to stone.

Other rock formations take the shape of a horse, a lion, a drum or a

Seven Star Cave, Guangxi

Described in ancient literature as a "world within a cave" and "Residence of Immortals", this incredibly beautiful cavern lies in the western slope of Putuo Mountain. It has been a popular and revered showpiece of the Guilin area since the Tang dynasty 1,300 years ago, and its walls bear many inscribed tributes by poets and scholars dating back to those days. Millions of years ago it was part of an underground river, raised and added to the scenic wonders of Guilin Province by a massive upheaval of the earth's surface. ▽

zither — all uncannily true to life.

The cave is illuminated, and visitors are able to take in an enjoyable tour which covers about 500 metres. △

Li River

Fishermen on bamboo rafts, their lamps lit to attract shoals of fish, add to the fairyland effect of the Li River and its most scenic stretch between Guilin and Yangshuo. The men use tamed cormorants to make their catches. The Li River, a principal tributary of the River Gwei, flows from Xing'an northwest of Guilin through to Yangshuo and then joins the West River after a distance of 437 kilometres.

Its waters are varied. The Guilin-Yangshou stretch is so placid that one can see the pebbles lying on the river bed. Elsewhere, the rapids can be difficult to negotiate.

The numerous, rugged peaks on the two sides of the meandering river offer a feast to the river traveller's eye. Yuan Mei, the Qing poet, marvelled at the swift-changing scenery and made the following observation of the river tour. "One moment, you see the green peaks floating over your head; the next, they glide under your boat." ▽

Chengyang Wind-Rain Bridge

Another striking example of a traditional covered bridge, this one was built by the Dong tribespeople to span the Linxi River in Sanjiang county. It was constructed in 1916 on a spot which has long been a meeting place of the Dong clans. Seventy-six metres long, it has five stone piers but otherwise is built entirely of wood. ▷

Flower Bridge (Huaqiao)

This elegant bridge reflects the traditional Han Chinese architecture and was rebuilt in 1540 in the time of the Ming rule at the confluence of the Small East River and Lingjian River in Guilin. It is 125 metres long, built of rock and actually extends way beyond the span of the river, with seven more arches besides the four that can be seen here. A green-tiled roof provides the "wind-rain" protection, but is not as dramatic as those of the Dong design. To the east of the bridge stands Hibiscus Rock, prettily named but actually a symbol of suffering: it bears the watermarks of many floods that have swept across the area in the past. ▷

Golden Cock Hill

These three boulders positioned high above the Wu River in Lechang County have for centuries been seen as a roosting cock — a fowl which, in Chinese belief and superstition, has the power to transform itself into a human being and wreak harm upon society if it so wishes. It is used in sacrifices, and certainly not eaten, its flesh regarded as unwholesome. Its crowing is said to be a sign of faithfulness, but if a hen crows it is taken as a sign of treachery. △

Seven-Star Cliffs

Rising abruptly from the northern district of Zhaoqing City in northwest Guangdong Province, these seven dramatic karst formations are arranged like the big dipper constellation and are reputed to bring together the magical forces of both the hills of Guilin and the West Lake of Hangzhou. The cliffs are also noted for the many caves at their bases, the most famous of them being Stone Chamber Cave which contains an underground river accessible by boat and many inscriptions on its walls dating back as far as the 6th century. Thirty years ago a small lake under the peaks was enlarged to provide irrigation and fish-breeding grounds, landscaped and beautified and named Star Lake. Bridges and pavilions were added in the Ming and Qing architectural styles. Zhaoqing itself goes back for more than 1,500 years and was formerly called Duanzhou. It is famous for its Duan inkstones and ivory carvings. ▷

Dinghu Mountain

Known simply as "the lake on a hill", this scenic spot northeast of Zhaoqing is said to be where the Yellow Emperor had a large bronze cooking vessel called a *ding* cast and installed. The area is abundant with rare plants and also features a series of picturesque waterfalls. An old monastery called Qingyun, constructed in 1633, stands at the foot of the hill. It once accommodated about 800 monks. Two large iron woks, called "thousand-people" woks, still hang in the monastery as evidence of its grander days.

△

Conghua Hot Springs

There are 140 hot spring sites in Guangdong Province, and Conghua, 75 kilometres from Guangzhou (Canton), is the most popular of them. Its waters are clear, odourless and "soft" — and their temperature ranges from a reasonably comfortably 30°C to 70°C. Nearby are three large waterfalls called Perfumed Powder, Flying Rainbow and Hundred Fathom. The source of the Hundred Fathom cascade is a body of water called Sky Lake in the hills above the resort. ▷

Danxia Mountain

Though not as dramatic as that of Guilin, the landscape of Guangdong Province includes similar karst formations in the same sort of idyllic river-valley settings. One of its most famous spots is Danxia Mountain, eight kilometres south of Renhua County, where the reddish (*dan*) colour of the soil contrasts attractively with the tropical green of the dense woodlands and the misty blue of the limestone range. An old monastery called Biechuan, built by the monk Tangui some 300 years ago, nestles among the limestone crags. ◁

Zhongshan Memorial Hall

This, the memorial to Guangdong Province's most famous son, Dr Sun Yatsen, stands on the southern slope of Yuexiu Hill in Guangzhou. The republican revolutionary assumed the style-name Zhongshan when he was installed as interim president of China in 1922 after his initial republican movement had struggled through chaos and civil unrest caused by the powerplay of various competing warlords.

The hall stands 49 metres high and the compound occupies an area of more than 4,700 square metres.

The octagonal memorial hall is palatial, and has a rich colour combination: vermilion columns, yellow walls and blue glazed tiles.

The hall seats over 4,000 people and there is not a single pillar to block anyone's view. Both the hall and the bronze statue of Dr Sun Yatsen were completed in 1931 from funds raised by overseas Chinese.

This is regarded by many as a masterpiece of modern Chinese architecture. △

Qinghui Garden

This splendid residence, situated in Shunde County, Guangdong Province and built in 1800, features a main house constructed in the "boat mansion" design — it looks like a traditional luxury houseboat from the outside — and is set among studios and pavilions in a water garden as fine as any found in the most celebrated centre of residential architecture, Suzhou. It reflects the wealth Guangdong and its neighbouring provinces enjoyed through trade and communication with foreigners. ▷

Foshan Ancestral Temple

This temple, first built in 1085 in the Song dynasty and originally called North King, is not a place of ancestral worship at all, but is called that because it is the oldest in Foshan City. Its main feature is a parade of beautifully sculptured ceramic figures along the ridges of its roofs, reflecting Foshan's long-standing reputation as a leading producer of porcelain and other ceramics. The temple was rebuilt in the Ming dynasty and consists of two main halls and the Tower of Rejoicing in Immortality, Pond of Splendid Fragrance and Stage of Myriad Blessings. Nearby is a park in which stands a Qing dynasty museum. ▷

West Lake of Huizhou

Lying by the side of Huizhou City in Guangdong Province, West Lake is as famous as a supplier of freshwater fish as it is for its placid beauty. It is also associated with the famous Song dynasty poet and calligrapher Su Shi (Su Dongpo) who was banished here and became prefect of the city. During his term of office he wrote these much-quoted lines extravagantly celebrating the distinctive southern fruit, the lychee:

"It's spring all year round
Below the Loufou Mountains.
Strawberries, loquats
Make their debut
One by one
And the lychees!
O, for three hundred lychees a
Day.
I do not mind
Spending all my days
South of the ranges."

▽

West Lake of Chaozhou

In the time of the Tang dynasty a long dyke was built in Chaozhou, separating the waters of the Han River. The enclosed area was landscaped and beautified, and today it is the city's West Lake. A popular recreation spot, it features double- and single-eaved pavilions and bridges connecting its various viewpoints and resting places.

▷

Guangji Bridge

Spanning the Han River in Chao-zhou, this bridge looks quite modern at first glance, but its stone arches to each side of the central steel span reveal its true age. It was first built in the 12th century, 515 metres long and constructed of granite blocks. The central span was added in this century to widen its access for modern river shipping. But its traditional form remains notable as one of the four greatest ancient bridges in China. ▽

World's End

The sombre-looking beach spot with its two huge boulders on the southern tip of Hainan Island was about as far as any Chinese official cared to go in ancient times. And even then, it meant shame. This was Tianyahaijiao, literally the End of the World, reflecting the view in those days that the civilised world ended on the borders of Chinese civilisation. When government officials found themselves posted to Hainan it was a sure sign that they had attracted extreme displeasure on the mainland. ▷

Hainan Island

Hainan, off the southernmost tip of China, is the second largest of the nation's 5,000 or more islands. Covering an area of 32,000 square kilometres, it is low-lying in the north and mountainous in the central region and south. Its tallest hills, the Five-Fingered Mountains, reach 1,879 metres and are clearly visible from the mainland 18 kilometres away. Most parts of the island are idyllic — lush forests and tropical beaches being among its charms. Elsewhere, in its fertile valleys, its mixed population of native Yi and Han Chinese settlers cultivate rice, rubber, coffee, tobacco, pepper and cocoa. Mahogany is one of its most famous products, traditionally used for furniture making as far away as Suzhou. The island also has large deposits of iron ore. ◁

Xisha Archipelago

Lying southeast of Hainan, this cluster of 30 small islands is famous for its largely undisturbed beauty. The chain is part of the South Sea Islands, which number more than 200. The group's central island is Yongxing, rich, like the others, in tropical produce such as bananas, papaya, coconuts and sugar cane. The group is also a natural sanctuary for birds, and thousands of them representing many species flock there all year round. ▽

Ten Thousand Rocks

This picturesque rock and lakeland setting is found in the Lion Hill resort area near Xiamen (Amoy) in Fujian Province. Nearby is a monastery called Ten Thousand Rock Lotus and a rock formation whose shape is vividly described by its name, Drunken Immortal Rock. Fujian, a mountainous coastal province facing Taiwan, was taken under the imperial Chinese wing in the Tang dynasty, and has been famous for its trading and emigration links with the outside world — and the huge overseas Chinese communities — since then.

◁

Mulan Dyke

Constructed in the 11th century, the now largely dilapidated dyke was a water conservation project built to control the floodwaters and to irrigate surrounding land where the Mulan River joins Xinghua Bay in Putian, Fujian. ◁

Nine Bend Stream

Typical of the scenic beauty of much of Fujian Province is the seven-kilometre stretch of rugged natural parkland in the Wuyi Range, through which the river flowing from Sanbao Mountain bends and twists nine times. Every bend presents the visitor with a different view — a waterfall here, an abruptly rising peak there, or an interesting rock formation. On the left bank of the fifth bend is a studio where Zhu Xi, a famous scholar of the Song dynasty, delivered his many lectures on philosophy.

Negotiating one's way down the meandering river on a bamboo raft is perhaps the most leisurely way of appreciating the breathtaking views which unfold one after another.

The Wuyi Mountains to the north of the province form the border with Jiangxi, and are regarded as being among the most attractive hills in China. ▽

Wuyi Range

The Wuyi Mountains extend for 250 kilometres through western Fujian Province. Since the Tang dynasty they have been a well-known Buddhist retreat. More than 100 monasteries have been built on their slopes and among the peaks, so that the 20th-century visitor will find a wealth of ancient architecture and relics. The mountains are also renowned for their Dahongpao tea, adding to the reputation of Fujian Province itself as one of China's paramount tea-producing areas. △

Luoyang Bridge

This bridge, extended by a cause-way to span reclaimed land, crosses the Luoyang River between Chuanzhou City and Hui'an County in Fujian. The bridge itself was built in 1053 and has 46 piers. First the piers of the bridge were formed in shallow water using fast-multiplying oysters as a cementing agent. Then large stone slabs were carried by boat and laid on the piers while the river tide was high.

There are 500 carved panels in the balustrades, 20 stone lions stand guard on either side, and the structure is decorated with nine stone pagodas. The entire crossing is 1,200 metres long.

The bridge was reinforced with cement and steel when Quanhui high-way was built in 1932, extending the width of the bridge from five to seven metres. ▷

320

Statue of Laojun

This massive stone sculpture of Laojun (Laotze), the founder of Taoism, stands on the slope of Wu Mountain in the northern area of Chuanzhou. It is one of very few surviving works of art in Fujian that date from the Song dynasty, when Chinese pictorial art and its celebration of nature reached its high point, and when, without coincidence, Taoism and its worship of man's relation to nature enjoyed an upswing too. The statue is five metres high and, naturally, is regarded as a masterpiece of the art of stonework. ◁

Kaiyuan Monastery

Originally called the Lotus Monastery, this place of worship and meditation in Chuanzhou City was first built in AD 686 in the reign of Ruizong of the Tang dynasty. Its architecture is strictly Han Chinese, yet it also points to the international contact that Fujian Province has maintained over the centuries. It features 72 panels of bas-relief carved with figures of lions with human heads, similar to the Egyptian Pharaonic style of artwork. It also has columns with cornices reminiscent of classical Greek architecture.   ▷

Shuzhuang Garden

This, the most popular garden in the famous Fujian port of Xiamen (Amoy), has two distinctive features. Just inside the main gate there is a shadow wall which was built there to deliberately highlight the scenery beyond — it keeps the visitor from seeing the sea at once, thus adding to the impact of the view. The garden also features a rockery which is considered one of the best in southern China. ◁

Sunshine Cliff

Sunshine Cliff is the highest point of Longtou Mountains, a range of hills on the coast of Fujian Province, near the city of Xiamen. A monastery by the same name lies on the slopes, while nearby are well-known scenic spots hidden among huge rocks and deep caverns. On a clear day visitors can see across the straits to Jinmen, an island belonging to nationalist Taiwan. At the close of the Ming and the beginning of the Qing dynasties, the famous general Zheng Chenggong used the cliff and its environs as a training ground for his navy as part of his plan to recover Taiwan from the Japanese. He is commemorated by a park, a gate preserved from his time, and inscriptions carved on the cliff face in bold calligraphy. ▽

Taiwan

This is the largest of all of China's islands, and has an area of 35,700 square metres. Lying just to the east off China's southern coast, it slumbered through much of the mainland's vast history, remaining relatively unnoticed beyond the sphere of Chinese affairs, and for a long time noted only for its natural resources and agricultural output. It was first colonised by the Dutch, and then taken by the Japanese in the 1870s and renamed Formosa. When World War Two ended in 1945, it was returned to mainland China after 50 years of Japanese occupation. When the Chinese Communists took over mainland China in 1949, the Nationalist (Kuomintang) government moved here and proclaimed Taipei its provisional capital, and since then no open contact with mainland China has been admitted.

Actually part of the mainland some millennia ago, Taiwan became an island when earth movements created the Taiwan Strait. Geologically it remained identifiable with the coastal regions of Fujian Province in eastern China. It is a hilly island, with a high central range running like a spine from north to south. The northern part is pockmarked with extinct volcanoes and surrounding hot springs. The highest peak, Yu Mountain,

rises west of the central range to a height of nearly 4,000 metres. Streams are mostly short and rapid. The western part of the island is a sedimentary plain, with many beaches lining its shores. This is the main farming region of the island, and supports 40% of the total population. In the east and the south the coastal plain is much narrower. Off the coast of this large island, 88 much smaller islands lie in different directions.

The tropical climate and plentiful rainfall make this region a regular producer of rice, sugar cane, tea and some 80 varieties of fruit. The forests in the hills are rich in red juniper, while camphor trees and their related produce come from the plains. There are also gold, silver, copper, coal and oil deposits. Fisheries are well developed along the shores. Industries and trading are concentrated in Taibei (Taipei), the capital, and the towns — Jilong, Taizhong, Tainan, Gaoxiong and Taidong.

This Treasure Island of China was noted for its Eight Scenic Sights and Twelve Wonderful Spots in the Qing dynasty. The hilly regions, caverns, shoreline and lake districts create a variegated landscape, while historical sites and relics are found mainly in the old town of Tainan in the southwest.   △

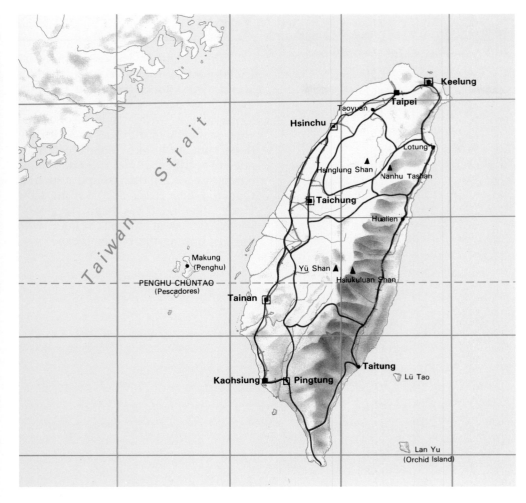

Cape Fugui

Part of Taibei (Taipei) County on the extreme northern tip of Taiwan, Cape Fugui is a transliteration of the Dutch word for "promontory". A feature is its rock formations along the shores, moulded into all sorts of interesting shapes by ancient volcanic eruptions and the strong seasonal northeast winds that buffet the coast. A 30 metre-high eight-cornered lighthouse warns shipping away from the rocky shelf. It was built in 1897. ▽

Yehliu

This, another rocky promontory 15 kilometres from Keelung, extends about two kilometres along the northern coast and, viewed from Keelung, looks like a turtle. It is also dotted with some 40 grotesque rock formations that look like idols erected by ancient tribespeople. Some have names which fit their shapes, such as Queen Head Rock and Resting Cow Rock. The area has been developed somewhat as a tourist venue, with bridges linking the bigger rocks. ◁▽

Zhinan Palace

Opulent, palatial, imperial — it is difficult to find words that fully encompass the strange grandeur of this spectacular Taoist temple in the southeastern suburbs of Taibei (Taipei). Standing on a hill with its roof of yellow tiles rising solemnly into the sky against a background of dense forest vegetation, Zhinan Palace, commonly known as Fairy Temple, was built in the year 1881 (the 7th year of the Qing emperor Guangxu), and houses the shrine of Lu Dongbin, one of Chinese Taoism's Eight Immortals. Said to be a scholar and recluse who lived around 750, Lu Dongbin is the patron saint of barbers and is worshipped by the sick and disabled. His emblem is a sword, with which he conquered various forms of evil throughout the world in a vendetta said to have lasted 400 years. The temple is also dedicated to the Jade Emperor and other Taoist deities, while a statue of Lu Dongbin attracts worshippers to the nearby Silver Stream Cave, an old temple erected over a natural cave and washed by a waterfall plunging from above. △

Shuangxi Park

Shuangxi (Double Stream) Park near Taibei (Taipei) was landscaped and beautified to the design of the famous residential gardens of Suzhou, and so successful has the copy proved that one almost expects to see retired mandarins strolling contentedly by its waters. ▷

Longshan Temple

An old structure, first built in 1738, more than a century before the coming of the Japanese, is Lungshan Temple southwest of Taipei. It was renovated in 1920 under Japanese supervision. The deities enshrined here include the goddess Guanyin, the Manjusri Bodhisattva, Pu Xian and 18 arhats. ▽

328

Sun Moon Lake

Lying in Nantou County and covering more than seven and a half square kilometres, Sun Moon Lake is the largest natural lake in Taiwan. It takes its name from its shape — the northern half is round like the sun and the southern section is crescent-shaped. It is a popular resort, with a summer temperature of about 22°C and a temperature in winter rarely falling below about 15°C. South of the lake there is a hill called Green Dragon where several monasteries stand. One of them contains relics which are said to be those of the Tang dynasty monk Tripitaka. ▽

Ali Mountain

One of the most memorable experiences in Taiwan is travelling to the summit (or summits) of Ali Mountain to watch the sun rise over its dramatic "sea of clouds". A railway, 72 kilometres long, takes visitors up the mountain range, climbing from tropical to temperate forest zones and travelling through 82 tunnels, the largest of which runs for 1,300 metres through the hillsides. At Ali Mountain's highest peak, Ta Mountain (2,600 metres), visitors stand in awe of the magnificent natural spectacle of clouds hanging hundreds of metres below them, billowing through ravines and over mountain crags and rolling in huge cottonwool waves in from the horizon. Zhu Mountain, its smaller sister, is the best place from which to watch the sunrise, first a faint red line on the eastern horizon, then a blood-red orb lifting out of the sea of clouds and finally a series of radiant beams of light. Ali Mountain's forests produce rare, high quality timber including Taiwan pine, China fir and Chinese juniper. In the spring, the range is full of cherry blossom. ▽

The Sacred Tree of Ali Mountain

High on Ali Mountain, central Taiwan's famous mountain stretch, stands a giant red Chinese juniper which is believed to be about 3,000 years old. It belongs to a species of trees found in Ali Mountain's virgin forests which grows at a very slow speed. Its bark gives out a pleasant aroma. Known as the Treasure of Ali Mountain, the juniper is not only astonishingly old, but also extraordinarily huge, measuring 53 metres in

height and with a girth of 20 metres. Having survived centuries of tremendous storms, forest fires and indiscriminate timber felling, it is now regarded as the god of trees, and is honoured in an inscription entitled "Ode to the Sacred Tree" carved on a stone plaque installed in a nearby wooden pavilion.

▷

Confucian Temple

This temple complex is said to have been built in 1666 in the reign of one of China's greatest imperial supporters and benefactors of the arts, Emperor Kangxi. And, as its name implies, it includes many shrines designed to commemorate the Confucian ethics of virtue, charity and duty to one's fellow man. Like Confucian temples throughout China it has red walls, an altar to the sage, a tablet inscribed with a tribute to his "most excellent spirit" and shrines to Famous Officials, Filial Sons, the Loyal and Filial and the Virtuous. ◁

Yu Mountain

Yu, or Jade Mountain, lies in the centre of Taiwan, its peaks rising to an average 2,000 metres. However, its principal peak, named after the range, towers to 3,970 metres, the highest in all of eastern China. In winter, the peaks are clad in two or three metres of snow. As with most of Taiwan's mountain areas, Yu Mountain has its recreation areas and resorts; a path zig-zags from the middle of the mountain to Paiyun Mountain Villa, a red-roofed stone guesthouse which overlooks a dramatic ravine. The path carries on from there, but the going is difficult with sections of it actually cut into the faces of the cliffs. On its higher reaches Yu Mountain features dense forests of white-wood. ◁

Oluanpi

Oluanpi, which is part of a coral reef area, is the southernmost tip of Taiwan, rising 122 metres out of the sea in the shape of a cape five metres long and 1-2.5 metres wide. It is one of two promontories identified on the eastern and western edges of the Hengcun Peninsula which jut out into the Pacific Ocean like the tail of a fish. Cat Nose is the name of the western promontory, while the name of the eastern promontory, Oluanpi, is the transliteration of the word "sail" in the language of the local indigenous Paiwan tribe. Oluanpi faces the island of Luzon in the distance, and commands the passageway between the South Sea and the Pacific Ocean.

A famous feature on Oluanpi is the lighthouse called Light of East Asia, built in 1882 (in the 8th year of the Qing emperor Guangxu). The biggest lighthouse in the Far East, it blinks once every 10 seconds and sheds its light seaward to a distance of 20 sea miles, signalling into what for many centuries was regarded as the mysterious, barbaric world lying beyond enlightened China. ▽

Index

Picture Credits & Acknowledgments

Front Cover: Nine Dragons Wall. Photo by Stephen Wong.
Back Cover: Mount Huangshan. Photo by K.K. Lau.
Endpapers: Murals from Kumbum Monastery. Photo by Peter Kwan. 1 Man-lork Chung. 2-3 Peter Kwan. 8-9 Peter Kwan. 11 Shiang-yang Liu. 12-13 Cheng-jian Yu. 13 George Chan. 14 Jacky Yip. 14-15 Peter Kwan/Jacky Yip Photography. 15 Ye Hsiao. 16 George Chan. 16-17 Shiang-yang Liu. 17 Manlork Chung. 18 Bo Chen. 18-19 Bo Chen. 20 Rebecca Lee. 20-21 Rebecca Lee. 21 Jacky Yip. 22 George Chan. 22-23 George Chan. 23 Sheang Kwan. 24 (top) Man-lork Chung; (bottom) Ming Miao. 25 Ming Miao. 26 (top) George Chan; (bottom) Ming Miao. 27 Ling Yuan. 28 Peter Kwan/Jacky Yip Photography. 28-29 Peter Kwan/Jacky Yip Photography. 29 Rebecca Lee. 30 Man-lork Chung. 30-31 (top) Peter Kwan/Jacky Yip Photography; (bottom) Man-lork Chung. 32 Ringo Mak. 32-33 George Chan. 33 George Chan. 34 (top) George Chan; (bottom) Ancient Chinese Architecture. 35 Man-lork Chung. 36 George Chan. 36-37 Jacky Yip. 37. Rebecca Lee. 38 George Chan. 39 (top) George Chan; (bottom) George Chan. 40-41 George Chan. 41 Mei Cheng. 42 Classical Chinese Gardens. 42-43 Ancient Chinese Architecture. 43 Classical Chinese Gardens. 44 Tiejun Shue. 44-45 Lian-sheng Chao. 45 Tie-jun Shue. 46 Liansheng Chao. 46-47 Tie-jun Shue. 47 Tie-jun Shue. 48 Yuhua Wei. 49 Da-lin Cheng. 50 Peter Kwan. 50-51 Jacky Yip. 51 (top) Da-lin Cheng; (bottom) Jacky Yip. 52 Da-lin Cheng. 53 (top) Georming Lee; (bottom) Georming Lee. 54 Jacky Yip. 55 Peter Kwan/Jacky Yip Photography. 56-57 Peter Kwan. 59 Chi-shan Cheng. 60 Chi-cai Yu. 60-61 Jacky Yip. 61 Jacky Yip. 62-63 Jacky Yip. 63 Peter Kwan. 64 Guang-kuan Li. 64-65 Jacky Yip. 65 Jacky Yip. 66-67 Jacky Yip. 67 Jacky Yip. 68 (top) Jacky Yip; (bottom) Jacky Yip. 69 Jacky Yip. 70 (top) Peter Kwan; (bottom) Peter Kwan. 71 Peter Kwan. 72 (top) Peter Kwan; (bottom) Jacky Yip. 73 Jacky Yip. 74-75 (top) Jacky Yip; (bottom) Jacky Yip. 75 Jacky Yip. 76 (top) Peter Kwan; (bottom) Peter Kwan. 77 Peter Kwan. 78 Peter Kwan. 78-79 Peter Kwan. 79 Jing-yeh Wang. 80 Jacky Yip. 80-81 Peter Kwan. 81 Jacky Yip. 82 (top) Da-lin Cheng; (bottom) Ringo Mak. 83 Classical Chinese Gardens. 84 Jacky Yip. 85 (top) Sheng-cai Li; (bottom) Water Poon. 86 Ji-ming Dai. 87 (top) Shou-kang Gu; (bottom) Jacky Yip. 88-89 Ke-chong Yuan. 89 Jacky Yip. 90 (top) Jacky Yip; (bottom) Song Kang. 91 Song Kang. 92 Song Kang. 92-93 Classical Chinese Gardens. 93 Classical Chinese Gardens. 94 (top) Shou-kang Gu; (bottom) Shou-kang Gu. 95 Shou-kang Gu. 96 Da-yi Liu. 96-97 Chi-shan Cheng. 97 Tian-ji Guan. 98 Ringo Mak. 99 Peter Kwan. 100 Shum Chow. 100-101 Da-lin Cheng. 101 Peter Kwan. 102 Ringo Mak. 102-103 Peter Kwan. 103 Peter Kwan. 104 Peter Kwan. 105 Peter Kwan. 106-107 Palaces of The Forbidden City. 109 Bu-tian Ding. 110 (top) Manlork Chung; (bottom) Chong-yi Ma. 111 Chong-yi Ma. 112 K.K. Lau. 113 (top) Bu-tian Ding; (bottom) Man-lork Chung. 114 (top) Jacky Yip; (bottom) George Chan. 115 (top) Jacky Yip; (bottom) Peter Kwan. 116 Li-men Yang. 116-117 Chen-hua Li. 117 Jacky Yip. 118 (top) Jacky Yip; (bottom) Roger Chung. 119 Jacky Yip. 120-121 Peter Kwan. 121 Peter Kwan/Jacky Yip Photography. 122 (top) K.K. Lau; (bottom) Peter Kwan/Jacky Yip Photography. 123 K.K. Lau. 124 Rong-gui Dong. 124-125 Peter Kwan. 126 George Chan. 127 Chen-hua Li. 128 Chen-sun Cheng. 128-129 Chen-sun Cheng. 129 Chen-sun Cheng. 130 Ancient Chinese Architecture. 131 (top) Ancient Chinese Architecture: (bottom) Peter Kwan. 132 (top) Peter Kwan/Jacky Yip Photography; (bottom) Peter Kwan/Jacky Yip Photography, 133 Rebecca Lee. 134 Roger Chung. 135 (top) Peter Kwan/Jacky Yip Photography; (bottom) Roger Chung. 136 (top) Peter Kwan; (bottom) Peter Kwan/Jacky Yip Photography. 137 George Chan. 138 Roger Chung. 139 (top) Butian Ding; (bottom) Bu-tian Ding. 140 Rebecca Lee. 140-141 Ancient Chinese Architecture. 141 Yue-nian Bi. 142 (left) Ancient Chinese Architecture; (right) Water Poon. 143 (top) George Chan; (bottom) Rebecca Lee. 144 Chen-hua Li. 144-145 Chen-hua Li. 146 Bin Chang. 147 (top) Derick Tse; (bottom) Man-lork Chung. 148 Peter Kwan. 148-149 Palaces of The Forbidden City. 150 (top) Chen-hua Li; (bottom) Man-lork Chung. 151 (top) Palaces of The Forbidden City; (bottom) Jacky Yip. 152 Ping-ching Wong. 152-153 Yuan Chen. 153 Thomas Tam. 154 Georming Lee. 154-155 Leung Yau. 155 Ancient Chinese Architecture. 156 (top) Jacky Yip; (bottom) Georming Lee. 157 (left) Shuyuan Chang; (right) Shu-yuan Chang. 158 Lian-suo Bai. 158-159 De-hua Gu. 159 George Chan. 160 (top) Man-lork Chung; (bottom) Ping-ching Wong. 161 (left) Hang Dong; (right) Hang Dong. 162 (top) Ancient Chinese Architecture; (bottom) Jacky Yip. 163 Ancient Chinese Architecture. 164 Ping-ching Wong. 165 Ancient Chinese Architecture. 166 (top) Ju-ce Han; (bottom) Jacky Yip. 167 Ju-ce Han. 168 (top) Chen-hua Li; (bottom) Chang-yuan Li. 169 Chang-yuan Li. 170 Classical Chinese Gardens. 171 (top) Wan Fung; (bottom) Mei-seong Wong. 172-173 Peter Kwan. 173 (top) Mei-seong Wong; (bottom) Mei-seong Wong. 174-175 Fou-li Tchan. 175 Fou-li Tchan. 176 (top) Mei-seong Wong; (bottom) Hong-man Tso. 177 Mei-seong Wong. 178 Mei-seong Wong. 178-179 Guo-fang Yue. 179 Jacky Yip. 180 Guo-fang Yue. 180-181 Jacky Yip. 182 (top) George Chan; (bottom) Peter Kwan. 183 George Chan/Jacky Yip Photography. 184 Yong Cheng. 184-185 Jacky Yip. 185 Liu-ren Chang. 186 Peter Kwan. 187 Jacky Yip. 188 Jacky Yip. 188-189 (top) Shum Chow; (bottom) Peter Kwan. 190 (top) George Chan; (bottom) Mei Cheng. 191 (top) Water Poon; (bottom) Water Poon. 192 Manly Chin. 192-193 Bak-kuen Mok. 193 Mei-seong Wong. 194-195 Peter Kwan. 197 Chu-fat Mak. 198 (top) Peter Kwan; (bottom) Li-chi Chin. 199 Li-chi Chin. 200 Peter Kwan. 201 (top) Stephen Wong; (bottom) Peter Kwan. 202 (top) Peter Kwan; (bottom) Wan Fung. 203 (top) Wan Fung; (bottom) Peter Kwan. 204 (top) Chen-hua Li; (bottom) Chu-fat Mak. 205 Jacky Yip. 206 (top) Chieh Chen; (bottom) Ringo Mak. 207 (top) Ringo Mak; (bottom) Jacky Yip. 208 Peter Kwan. 208-209 Peter Kwan. 209 Peter Kwan. 210 Jacky Yip. 210-211 Peter Kwan. 211 Jacky Yip. 212 Peter Kwan. 213 (top) Peter Kwan; (bottom) Classical Chinese Gardens. 214 (top) Shun-chi Chin; (bottom) Jacky Yip. 215 Jacky Yip. 216 (top) Kuang-chien Ning; (bottom) Wai-leung Chak. 216-217 Wai-leung Chak. 218 George Chan. 218-219 George Chan. 219 George Chan. 220 George Chan. 220-221 George Chan. 221 George Chan. 222 (top) Cheng-jian Yu; (bottom) Cheng-jian Yu. 222-223 Cheng-jian Yu. 223 Cheng-jian Yu. 224 George Chan. 224-225 George Chan. 225 George Chan. 226 (top) Chen-hua Li; (bottom) Jacky Yip. 226-227 George Chan. 227 George Chan. 228 Jacky Yip. 229 (top) Jacky Yip; (bottom) Jacky Yip. 230 George Chan. 230-231 Jacky Yip. 231 Jacky Yip. 232 (top) George Chan; (bottom) Peter Kwan/Jacky Yip Photography. 223 Chen-hua Li. 234 George Chan. 234-235 George Chan. 235 Ching Mu. 236 Jacky Yip. 236-237 George Chan. 237 George Chan. 238 Fei Yang. 239 (top) Jacky Yip; (bottom) Fei Yang. 240 Yong Cheng. 240-241 George Chan. 241 George Chan. 242 (top) George Chan; (bottom) Peter Kwan. 243 (top) George Chan; (bottom) George Chan. 244 Yun-feng Chu. 244-245 George Chan. 245 George Chan. 246 George Chan. 247 (top) Chen-hua Li; (bottom) George Chan. 248 (top) Peter Kwan/Jacky Yip Photography; (bottom) Peter Kwan/Jacky Yip Photography. 249 Peter Kwan/Jacky Yip Photography. 250-251 Peter Kwan/Jacky Yip Photography. 251 Peter Kwan. 252 Man-lork Chung. 252-253 Man-lork Chung. 253 Georming Lee. 254-255 Peter Kwan. 255 Ancient Chinese Architecture. 256 George Chan. 256-257 George Chan. 257 Man-lork Chung. 258 Man-lork Chung. 258-259 Man-lork Chung. 259 Man-lork Chung. 260 Man-lork Chung. 261 (top) Man-lork Chung, (left bottom) Man-lork Chung; (right bottom) Man-lork Chung. 262 Yong Cheng. 263 Ping-ching Wong. 264 Man-lork Chung. 265 (top) George Chan; (bottom) Jacky Yip. 266 (top) George Chan; (bottom) Roger Chung. 267 Ping-lun Chiu. 268-269 (top) Liang Pak; (bottom) Peter Kwan. 270 Bang Hsu. 270-271 Bang Hsu. 271 Bang Hsu. 272 Peter Kwan. 273 Jacky Yip. 274 (top) Peter Kwan; (bottom) Jacky Yip. 275 R. Wada/Courtesy Lindblad Travel, Inc. 276 Cu-cheng Wu. 277 (top) Peter Kwan; (bottom) Peter Kwan. 278 Ringo Mak. 278-279 George Chan. 279 Ringo Mak. 280-281 Peter Kwan. 283 Yu-hu Chu. 284 (top) George Chan/Jacky Yip Photography; (bottom) Tian-fu Hsiang. 285 Yu-long Li. 286 George Chan/Jacky Yip Photography. 286-287 Manly Chin. 287 George Chan. 288-289 George Chan/Jacky Yip Photography. 289 Fu-chuan Min. 290-291 Manly Chin. 291 Chen-hua Li. 292 (top) Yu-long Li; (bottom) George Chan/Jacky Yip Photography. 293 George Chan. 294 (top) George Chan; (bottom) George Chan. 295 (top) George Chan; (bottom) Chen-hua Li. 296 George Chan. 296-297 Jacky Yip. 298 (top) George Chan; (bottom) George Chan. 299 George Chan. 300-301 Mau-king Chen. 301 Ya-jiang Chan. 302 (top) Jacky Yip; (bottom) Peter Kwan/Jacky Yip Photography. 302-303 Gui-ching Chou. 304-305 Mau-king Chen. 305 Rebecca Lee. 306 Gui-ching Chou. 307 (top) George Chan; (bottom) Wen-jun Yin. 308 Roger Chung. 308-309 Rebecca Lee. 310 George Chan. 310-311 Rebecca Lee. 311 Chi-sheng Chiang. 312 Rebecca Lee. 313 (top) George Chan; (bottom) Classical Chinese Gardens. 314 Jacky Yip. 314-315 Ying-ching Choy. 315 Man-lork Chung. 316 (top) Jacky Yip; (bottom) Jacky Yip. 317 Chong-chang Fu. 318 (top) Ancient Chinese Architecture; (bottom) George Chan. 319 George Chan. 320 Jacky Yip. 321 (top) Jacky Yip; (bottom) George Chan. 322 (top) Rebecca Lee; (bottom) Chi-keung Chan. 323 Rebecca Lee. 324 Norman Lau. 325 George Chan. 326 (top) Wai-kin Che; (bottom) Norman Lau. 327 George Chan. 328 Jacky Yip. 328-329 Norman Lau. 329 George Chan. 330-331 Norman Lau. 331 Norman Lau. 332 (top) Hsi-sheng Lee; (bottom) Wai-kin Che. 333 George Chan.

The publishers wish to express their gratitude to the following persons for contributing text to this book:
Tim-cheong Lai, Karen Lee, Carol Wai-yi Chan, Diana Yu, Rebecca Wing-kam Au.
The publishers also wish to thank Rand McNally & Company for permission to reproduce their maps in this book.